✳ Smithsonian

BIRDWATCHING GUIDE

TURN YOURSELF INTO A BIRDWATCHING EXPERT

☀ Smithsonian

BIRDWATCHING GUIDE

TURN YOURSELF INTO A BIRDWATCHING EXPERT

Contents

DK | Penguin Random House

Editor Annie Moss
Senior art editor Jessica Tapolcai
Managing editor Angeles Gavira Guerrero
Managing art editor Michael Duffy
Production editor Rob Dunn
Senior production controller Meskerem Berhane
US senior editor Jennette ElNaggar
Publishing director Georgina Dee
Art director Maxine Pedliham
Managing director Liz Gough
Design director Phil Ormerod

Produced for DK by
Designer Ali Scrivens
Authors Elissa Wolfson, Stephen W. Kress, Rob Hume

First American Edition, 2025
Published in the United States by
DK Publishing, a division of Penguin
Random House LLC
1745 Broadway, 20th Floor,
New York, NY 10019

A catalog record for this book is available from the Library of Congress.
ISBN 978-0-5939-6356-2

DK books are available at special discounts when purchased in bulk for sales promotions, premiums, fund-raising, or educational use. For details, contact: DK Publishing Special Markets, 1745 Broadway, 20th Floor, New York, NY 10019
SpecialSales@dk.com

Printed and bound in China
www.dk.com

MIX
Paper | Supporting responsible forestry
FSC™ C018179

This book was made with Forest Stewardship Council™ certified paper – one small step in DK's commitment to a sustainable future.
Learn more at www.dk.com/uk/ information/sustainability

Introduction

It could be the tuneful call of a hidden backyard visitor,
a curious shape flying overhead, or a lustrous feather found
on the ground that signals the fascinating world of birds.

On a sunny day in the park, you may spot a soaring red-tailed hawk against a fine blue sky. You could be spending an evening downtown and catch a glimpse of a nighthawk. Or just enjoying an afternoon in the backyard, you can hear the robins, see a flash of a bluebird's azure back, or watch swallows and martins speeding overhead. Wherever you are, there will be birds, and appreciating them can bring you a welcome sense of calm and delight.

Getting more curious about these sightings—what bird is it? How does it live?—can enrich your life in so many ways. Think about what you are seeing. How can that tiny scrap of life migrate thousands of miles each spring and return in the fall, seemingly never losing its way? How are there so many kinds of beautifully patterned warblers? And how do you correctly identify a bird given that many change color and develop new patterns as they age and the seasons change?

At first, identifying birds might seem daunting. But the only real rule to birdwatching is to not disturb the birds, and the only requirement is to be curious about what you can see and hear. And while birding can be a solitary pursuit, it also offers the chance to meet people, enjoy the company of others, and work things out together. It can be a great way to socialize.

Anyone can birdwatch, and it is almost completely free. Binoculars help, but there is little else you need except a good field guide. Birdwatching can take you anywhere—if you want to, you can join a club, collect bird books, search the internet, amass a collection of photographic gear, sketch what you see, or even record bird calls and songs. You might one day travel the world searching for birds. Birdwatching opens up so many opportunities: just look, listen, spare a few moments of your time, and enjoy.

Field skills and equipment

Birds can be seen all around us, but seeing is only part of the story—learn how to really look at birds and watch their behavior, then you'll fall completely in love with them.

What you need

The only investment you need for birdwatching is a little bit of time. Any other skills or equipment you acquire will enhance your experience, but the most important thing is patience.

Getting started

This chapter outlines a few simple skills that can help you make the most of your time birdwatching and walks you through some of the first steps toward buying equipment that will enhance your experience. Don't be put off by thinking you need expensive binoculars, cameras, or camouflage clothing. In many cases, it's not about what you've got but how you use it, and often there are very simple and relatively cheap ways in which you can modify something you might already have, such as a smartphone, to boost it into a birding aid. But if you do decide to invest, there's guidance to help you understand the options and make informed choices.

Gateway to a fascinating world

Just as you don't need a lot of equipment, you also don't need to invest huge amounts of time or travel to learn the skills. Birds are probably all around you, wherever you live, as they can make their home in all manner of habitats. There are simple techniques you can practice in your garden or park so that, if you then want to head off exploring the local parks and nature reserves or further afield, you'll be ready to make the most of your trip. And when you get there, our tips will help you navigate the new territory and step further into the wonderful world of birding. The more you learn, the more you see; and the more you see, the more you'll want to learn.

Install bird feeders so you can practice your bird identification skills

Getting close to birds
As well as going to the birds, you can also encourage them to come to you.

What to wear

The good news is that there are no rules and no special clothing required, so just wear clothing appropriate to the conditions. It's more important to be quiet than it is to wear camouflage clothing.

You can't hide from birds

Birds have acute binocular vision and will notice you before you see them, so moving quietly and unobtrusively is more useful than wearing special clothing to blend into the background. Bright colors won't scare birds off, but loud noises and unpredictability will. Noisy, rustling clothes are not ideal, as they can give you away. While military-style camouflage is unnecessary, it is worth avoiding colors that stand out from your surroundings if you're trying to get close in order to take photographs.

It's more important to be practical and pragmatic than to equip yourself with special gear, especially if you're birdwatching as a family; children grow out of waterproof clothing quickly, so it's worth considering buying secondhand too—not just from a budget point of view but also for ethical considerations of environmental impact. And should you want to exercise maximum consumer power, check that no environmentally harmful chemicals have been used in the waterproofing of any garments you buy.

Dress for the conditions

The important thing is to be dry and comfortable, so make sure you wear clothing and footwear appropriate for the conditions and terrain. Using binoculars, smartphone, or a telescope in cold weather can expose your fingers to the elements, so you might want to invest in gloves that work with a touchscreen. Large pockets are invaluable; they allow you to have things conveniently at hand, such as a phone, drinks, field guide, and snacks.

A hat with a brim will restrict glare

Protect your head
Wear a hat to shield your head from the sun or insulate from cold.

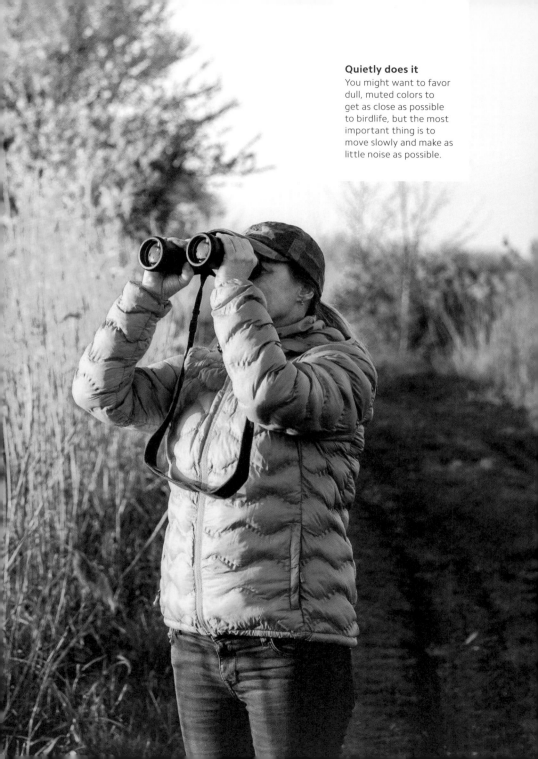

Quietly does it
You might want to favor dull, muted colors to get as close as possible to birdlife, but the most important thing is to move slowly and make as little noise as possible.

Observing from a blind

Public bird blinds offer shelter, good views across interesting habitats, and the chance to see birds close-up without disturbing them. Blinds are also great places to meet other birdwatchers.

Visiting a blind

Blinds are fixed shelters that allow you to watch birds close-up without scaring them off. The birds will know you're there, but because there are none of the dangers they associate with unpredictability, they feel safe and will generally just go about their business. Blinds often have bench seats and windows, with folding shutters and a shelf. There is usually space for 10–20 people seated, plus standing room behind them for more if the blind gets busy. Hanging out in a blind is a great way to learn to birdwatch, both for practicing your observation skills and developing identification techniques.

Blind etiquette

In a blind, you may be surrounded by like-minded enthusiasts from whom you can learn a great deal, so engage with the generosity of that community. There may be a bulletin board listing recent sightings to watch out for, for example, and regular visitors may be happy to share their local knowledge, but do be mindful of and

respect others within the blind who might be trying hard to listen to the birds outside.

If several people have tripods, things can get awkward, thanks to the high numbers of legs and feet—both of equipment and of people. If you're using a tripod in a blind that gets busy, it might be a good idea to take your scope or camera off the tripod and rest it on the sill, using a small clamp or beanbag to hold it still (see pp. 26–27). And if you see something interesting through your lens, offer to share your equipment so others can see it, too, making sure that everyone gets at least a quick look, in case the bird flies away.

Don't be afraid to ask questions, either—after all, you're among fellow bird lovers!

> A blind often allows you to observe birds without disturbing them

Wheelchair users can get close to windows thanks to recesses under the sills

Access for all
Some blinds have gently sloping ramps for wheelchair access and lower windows or sills.

Types of binoculars

Binoculars magnify what you see and get you closer to the action.
With such a wide selection available, it's worth taking the time to make
sure you find the right type for you, so ideally try before you buy.

Exploring the options

Binoculars range from tiny compact models to heavy ones with powerful magnification. Many have rubber or waterproof casings for protection. Lenses are usually coated to reduce reflected light and to give a brighter image.

Because the objective lenses of binoculars invert the image being viewed, they contain prisms to turn the image right-side up again. There are two arrangements of prisms: modern roof-prism designs, which can be expensive but are relatively lightweight and robust, with internal focusing controls that help protect them from the elements; and the traditional porro-prism option, which can be less expensive, but is usually bulkier, heavier, and more fragile.

Try them out to find which ones fit your budget and needs; you need to balance ease of use and magnification against weight and price. Think about buying secondhand, too, which can make your budget stretch further. And if buying new, do a bit of research if for ethical reasons you want to avoid manufacturers that support trophy hunting.

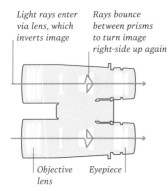

Light rays enter via lens, which inverts image *Rays bounce between prisms to turn image right-side up again*

Objective lens *Eyepiece*

Roof-prism binoculars
Comparatively light and easy to use, with a narrow, smooth shape.

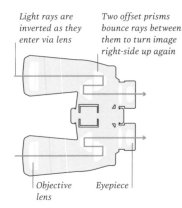

Light rays are inverted as they enter via lens *Two offset prisms bounce rays between them to turn image right-side up again*

Objective lens *Eyepiece*

Porro-prism binoculars
As the objective lenses are wider apart than the eyepieces, the binoculars have a "stepped" shape.

Check out secondhand options to help both your budget and the planet

Ready for a close-up
Binoculars must be light
enough to carry, easy to
use, and work well—
especially if you want
a young child to enjoy
birdwatching too.

Choosing binoculars

Once you've decided which design you find easiest to use, you then need to find the perfect compromise between magnification, brightness, and price. The best are expensive, but there are many good, relatively cheap (or secondhand) options on the market.

What do the numbers mean?

Binoculars are described by two numbers, such as "8x30" or "10x50." The first number refers to the magnification: i.e., 8 times or 10 times actual size. For birdwatching, anything between 7 and 12 can be useful, with 8 or 10 probably best. The second number relates to the diameter (in millimeters) of the larger (objective) lenses.

Comparative brightness

Larger objective lenses let in more light to give a brighter image. So 7x50 will give a brighter image than 7x30. But 7x50 will be brighter than 10x50, as the brightness of an image depends on the size of the "exit pupil," the light entering the eyepieces. The higher the exit pupil number, the brighter the image. To figure out the exit pupil size, divide the lens diameter by the magnification of the eyepiece.

$$\frac{50}{7} = 7.1\text{mm}$$

However, the quality of modern prisms, lenses, and coatings can enhance exit pupil calculations, and the best binoculars are superbly bright and clear with a very sharp image, even with a small exit pupil size, so you need to try them and compare.

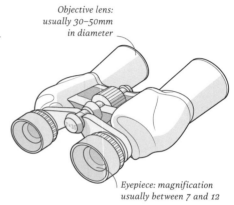

Objective lens: usually 30–50mm in diameter

Eyepiece: magnification usually between 7 and 12

An exit pupil size of 7.1mm (7x50) will let in plenty of light, to give a bright image

With an exit pupil size of 5mm (10x50), less light is gathered, so the image is duller

Size versus brightness

In many situations, brightness is not a major consideration, but in cloudy weather, on winter afternoons, or deep inside a dark forest, a brighter image is invaluable.

Relative magnification

You ideally want a close view, of course, but be aware: the higher the magnification, the more difficult it is to get a steady image, as you may experience "hand shake," although some models offer stabilization sensors. A higher magnification also gives a smaller field of view; you see a narrow area rather than a broader view—great if you are looking hard at one bird, but a wider view makes it easier to find the bird in the first place. For general birdwatching, anything up to a magnification of 10 is fine.

At high magnification, you get great detail but need a tripod or other support to hold binoculars steady

x20

Some designs have image stabilization to reduce shaking even at higher magnifications

At low magnification, you get a wide view of the scene but less detail, such as missing the number of lines on the puffin's beak

x10

x7

This magnification is clear and bright, and you can see some of the detail of the bill pattern

Using binoculars

Binoculars are easy to set up and use, but it's worth taking a bit of time to practice and familiarize yourself with the moving parts. Follow the simple steps below to get the best out of them.

What does what

Binocular barrels pivot in the middle so you can get the right angle and width for your eyes. Many people have one eye sharper than the other, "weaker" one. If you do, you need to "balance" any difference with binoculars, just as you would if you wear eyeglasses. To do this, there is an eyepiece adjuster on one barrel, which you set up once (but do check regularly that it hasn't moved).

Then there is a larger central focusing wheel, which you will need to adjust constantly. The main focus is set according to distance, so you'll need to move the focusing wheel every time you fix on a new object.

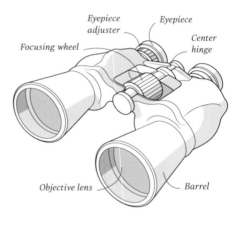

Eyepiece adjuster

Eyepiece

Center hinge

Focusing wheel

Objective lens

Barrel

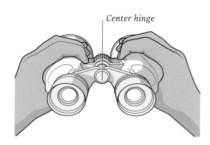

Center hinge

1. First, set the distance between the eyepieces. This distance needs to match the gap between your eyes. To adjust, just widen or squeeze the two barrels on either side of the center hinge.

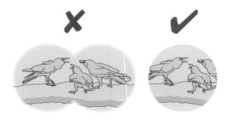

2. Adjust the width between the two barrels until you see a single, sharp-edged circle. You should never see a "figure eight" with soft or blurred edges.

Adjusting for eyeglasses

Most binoculars have eyecups that can be raised or pushed down, but many people simply raise their glasses up without adjusting the eyecups. If you decide to use the eyecups with glasses, push the eyecups down and press them against your glasses. The view will be similar, but light may intrude from the side. This can be blocked out by cupping your hands around the eyecups.

Eyecup flipped up

Eyecup flipped down

What suits you?

If you wear glasses, experiment with different ways of using your binoculars to see what feels most natural.

Keep your eyes relaxed— use the focusing wheel to get things in focus instead of straining your eyes

Focusing wheel

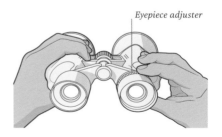

Eyepiece adjuster

3. Use the central focusing wheel to bring the subject sharply into focus. Relax your eyes, and focus on something that has sharp edges, such as a tree trunk or fence post.

4. Next, cover the left lens, keep both eyes open, and adjust the right eyepiece. Turn it right out of focus, then slowly bring it back until the image is sharp. Note the setting and keep it there.

Practice with binoculars

The more you practice using binoculars, even just in your yard, the more you'll become familiar with them. Soon using binoculars will become second nature, like blinking or walking.

Practice makes perfect

Follow the steps below to practice spotting birds, first focusing on a distant object, then on birds too. A garden or balcony bird feeder is an ideal practice zone, and you'll quickly learn to "hit the target" without needing to look down at the binoculars or move your head and eyes away from the bird.

Keep your binoculars in a case when not in use, but leave the case behind when you are out with them. Do strap them around your neck, however—you don't want to drop them. When using binoculars, it's a good idea to shorten the strap so that they hang high on your chest, closer to your face; when you're walking along with them not in use, lengthen the strap again and put one arm through so you can tuck them under your arm for protection and prevent them from flapping around. Use a cover to shield the eyepieces, and look after the lenses—if you have to clean them, just use a soft cloth, very gently; dirt around the edges can be cleaned with a fingernail pressed through the cloth.

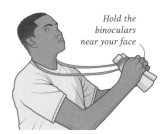

Hold the binoculars near your face

Keep your head still as you lift them up

1. With binoculars poised, scan a location with the naked eye. Have the strap short, so that when you're not holding them they hang high on your chest rather than down on your tummy.

2. When you see a bird, keep your eyes on it as you raise the binoculars to your face. Without moving your head or eyes, use your fingers to adjust the focusing wheel so the bird is in focus.

Still and steady
Hold binoculars firmly, with thumbs underneath, and let the weight settle into your hands, without gripping them too tightly. To avoid "hand shake," brace a finger against forehead and cheek. To block out unwanted light from the side, wrap your hands around the eyepieces.

Choosing a scope

Sometimes, if birds are far off, you might want to go beyond binoculars for higher magnification. Choosing a scope requires a similar approach to choosing binoculars—try to find the sweet spot that works for you between magnification, brightness, and price.

Why use a scope?

Much the same applies to telescopes as to binoculars (*see pp. 18–19*). The objective lens size can vary, and magnification may be fixed, or you can have a zoom lens that gives a range. If you want to travel light, you can just use a pocket-sized scope, but it won't be as powerful as a bigger lens. The bigger the lens, however, and the more light it lets in, the larger and heavier the scope has to be. The higher the magnification, the smaller the field of view and the more it becomes vital to avoid shake by using a tripod or other support. Again, as with binoculars, buying secondhand can be a good option.

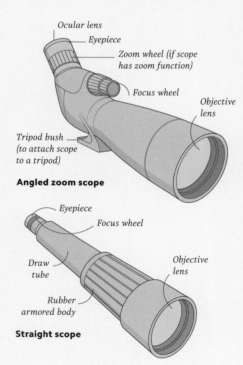

Ocular lens

Eyepiece

Zoom wheel (if scope has zoom function)

Focus wheel

Objective lens

Tripod bush
(to attach scope
to a tripod)

Angled zoom scope

Eyepiece

Focus wheel

Draw tube

Objective lens

Rubber armored body

Straight scope

Which is right for you?

A fixed 20x or 30x is a good option, or a zoom, such as 15–30x or 20–60x. Magnification affects the clarity of the image, so try out different strengths and zoom eyepieces before you buy.

There are two types of scopes: straight and angled. A straight scope is easy to use—you just line it up directly with the bird. You may need a bit more practice before you can easily line up an angled scope on a bird, but if you're trying to watch a bird high in the sky, for example, you'll soon appreciate the advantages of an angled eyepiece. Looking down into it may seem difficult at first, but it's really much more comfortable, especially for your neck. It's also a more practical option when sharing a scope with others, such as taller and shorter members of a family.

Pocket power
A compact scope that fits into your pocket can give you a good view without having to carry lots of gear.

Choosing a tripod
Factor the cost of a good tripod into your budget; a pan-and-tilt one with a single handle is ideal.

An angled scope is great for sharing sightings with people of different heights

How to use a scope

How quickly you get used to your scope depends on which one you've chosen—angled scopes require a little practice at first to find a bird, and higher magnifications need support to avoid shake.

Using your scope

There's no eyepiece wheel, just one or two focus wheels to adjust for distance, which you can fine-tune as you watch. Always keep your eye in line with the eyepiece or the image will not be clear. If you can, try to alternate eyes; after using one eye for several minutes, you may find it doesn't focus properly for a while. You can also avoid eyestrain by keeping both eyes open as you look through the scope, learning to "ignore" what the naked eye

is seeing. Most importantly, don't be a "scope hog"—if you see an interesting bird, let everyone have a quick look, then another longer look if there's time before the bird flies away.

Supporting your scope

There are several options for keeping your scope steady (*see below*). To stabilize yourself against the scope, rest one hand on the eyepiece, with one finger on the focus wheel and another braced against your forehead or nose. Ideally, arrange the three legs of your tripod so that two are positioned forward and one backward, between your legs.

Lock and release
Many tripods have a lock and release method that uses a quick-release plate to attach a scope.

A stable platform for your scope
Simple options include using a tripod, balancing the scope on a beanbag, or fixing it to a clamp with a tripod head.

Rest the scope on a beanbag

Use a clamp fixed to a sill, fence, or car window

Adjust a tripod to suit the viewing angle and terrain

Tripod skills
Learn to adjust the tilt-control lever of your tripod without taking your eye away from the eyepiece, to follow the action and pan more easily across a landscape.

Choosing photography equipment

Taking a photo of a bird for identification and recording purposes is very different from capturing a professional-looking photograph—but it's a lot cheaper and easier too!

First steps

This is not a detailed guide on how to use an expensive camera with a huge telephoto lens; we're focusing here on practical, convenient ways to capture good images of the birds you see, where possible just using equipment you probably have in your pocket—with perhaps just a few clever extras.

Using a smartphone, for example, allows you to share your photos instantly, and they can also be tagged, dated, and geolocated

Always ready
With a smartphone, you can quickly capture a shot whenever an opportunity arises and share it if you have cell service.

Improvised zoom
Hold your phone against a binocular eyepiece to take a close-up photo through the lens.

instantaneously. With a few extra add-ons, too, you can turn your smartphone into a zoom camera: a clip-on telephoto lens can get you much closer to the action, for example, or you can put your phone into an adapter that allows you to take photos directly through a scope (known as "digiscoping"). The higher a scope's magnification, the more using a tripod for stability will help avoid "hand shake".

Taking it further

If you want to invest further, a so-called "bridge camera" is a good place to start. These can be relatively cheap and lightweight, and often the sensors capture so much detail in the image that, as well as using its zoom lens, you can crop into the image for an even better close-up too.

Another option, if your interest in photographing birds continues to grow, is to adapt a window of your home to become a bird blind. Open a window facing the bird feeders in your yard and cover the opening with cloth that has one hole for a camera and another for viewing.

There are so many clever ways to adapt technology you probably already have to take great bird photos

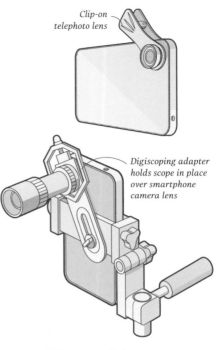

Clip-on telephoto lens

Digiscoping adapter holds scope in place over smartphone camera lens

Using a smartphone
Clip-on attachments, holders, and apps allow you to give your smartphone a zoom lens.

A built-in zoom lens is practical and convenient

Using a bridge camera
A bridge camera often has a fairly powerful zoom lens and can be controlled manually or automatically.

Photographing birds

Even with simple-to-use equipment, you'll need a bit of practice to make sure you're getting your birds center stage. And where better to start than your own balcony or garden?

A home bird blind

Set up a bird feeder outside a window of your home to turn it into a makeshift blind, and practice taking photos of the birds that visit you. Tailor the food you put out to bring a variety of birds to the feeder. Or visit a local park or nature reserve if you don't have a garden (many nature reserves have blinds set up with feeders nearby).

Practicing locally helps you become familiar with how to use the camera controls and attachments to capture the bird nicely. And if you're using a smartphone, the volume-down control on your headphones can sometimes be used as a remote shutter release to avoid tapping the phone screen to take a shot.

To take it to the next level, you can "stage-manage" your setup so that the feeder is placed in a particular setting, or against a particular backdrop, that will give you a superb photograph of your visitors. Not only will you be familiarizing yourself with your camera setup, but you'll also become better at anticipating bird behavior. If you have a setting for shallow depth of field, use that to blur out the background. Here and overleaf are a couple of examples you could try.

On a wooden log

To entice a red-headed woodpecker to a window blind, create a fake woodland of birches smeared with fat and seeds.

1. Create a woodland scene by hanging birch logs in front of a plain backdrop.

2. Add food—in this case, seeds stuck onto the logs with fat. Make sure the food is not visible in your camera angle.

3. Wait for your visitor, like this red-headed woodpecker, to arrive and take your photographs.

On a moss post
This moss-covered post was placed outside a window with seeds scattered on it. A nearby feeder ensured that birds were already regular visitors to the area.

1. Set the "stage" outside a window so you can watch from inside, possibly through drawn curtains.

2. Position the post in front of a simple green backdrop, and adjust the angle as necessary to fill the screen of your shot.

3. Sprinkle seeds on the sculpture and wait for a bird to arrive, such as this black-capped chickadee.

Next steps

As you become more proficient, you may want to start experimenting with composition, trying close-up details, for example, or action shots of birds in flight. Most bird photos look better if the eye is in focus, so for a "professional" touch when taking close-ups, focus on the eye, or at least the head. It can be hard to get everything sharp in a "head-on" shot, as the head and tail may be a long way apart and the depth of focus much smaller; to get the bird more completely in focus, a side view is best—but that may be the least attractive or creative view.

In close-ups, try to get the bird's eye in focus

If your camera allows you to set a shallow depth of field, you can have sharp focus in one area and soft blur elsewhere

Use a shutter speed of at least 1/2,500 second to capture birds in flight

Be organized

Get into the habit of backing up the photos you want to keep—and deleting the ones you don't (the environment is already paying the price for huge databanks of all the images we're taking, so don't keep photos you don't want).

You can use cloud storage, but it's worth also keeping a separate backup hard drive. Keep photos organized, too, with geolocation and other tags so that you can search on key words, places, dates, and bird species, or a system of folders so you can find things.

Using digital tools

It's not cheating to let the internet help you learn birding. There are some fantastic apps out there that can help you identify birds and their calls, and connect with the wider birding world.

Websites and e-guides

The internet is a wonderful teaching aid. It opens up a multitude of opportunities and gives you comprehensive information at your fingertips. There are myriad websites that can offer assistance in identifying a bird, and should you want to travel light rather than carry an identification guide; you can simply download an e-guide onto your smartphone. Your e-guide may also have links to video and audio, to help confirm that a bird species is what you think it is.

Apps and other e-tools

Sophisticated smartphone apps can help you identify a bird from just a picture or pick up its song and identify it from that for you. Attachments can enhance your phone's audio capacity, too. The apps are amazing—but they're not infallible. You need to sense-check what an app is telling

you if, for example, it's suggesting something completely inappropriate for the season, habitat, or location. Often, you'll hear a bird before you see it, but even if an app has told you what you can hear, look for a sighting tool to help the information "stick"; you won't actually learn how to identify birds independently unless you look and listen for yourself. What might you expect to see? Can you hear anything familiar? Test yourself and then confirm your sightings/soundings with the apps instead of just relying on them—that way you'll learn much more.

Be careful to choose websites, apps, and e-guides that are appropriate for your geographical location, and don't just rely on the internet. After all, you may not always have access to a reliable signal connection, or you may run out of battery (although it's always a good rule to carry a spare power pack to help on that score).

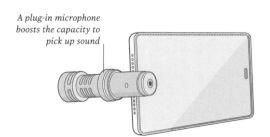

A plug-in microphone boosts the capacity to pick up sound

Audio accessories
You can fit a compact directional microphone to your smartphone. You may also want to use a furry windshield to reduce noise.

At your fingertips
Look at websites, e-guides, and your own photos to study the details of a bird: the shape of the head and beak; the color of the legs; and details of the plumage.

Keeping notes

Using your phone to track your sightings and soundings as you go allows you to keep a log of what you find. You can adjust your smartphone's setting to geotag and date all photos and keep a record of what you encounter. Often, there's a facility within apps and e-guides for you to add your own metadata tags and notes, too—but remember to back up all your information regularly, or keep a little notebook of your birding activity to help you remember what you've seen.

When you're out birdwatching, remember to give yourself time to just observe the birds—indulge your curiosity and wonder

A place for paper

Sometimes "analog" can be a good option instead of, or alongside, digital. Despite all the wonders of the internet, a good field guide is still a convenient reference tool, especially if you're in a bird blind for the day, as it won't run out of battery power, doesn't have a screen that can be hard to read in the glare of full sun, is easy to share with others, and gives you more of an overview of birds in a habitat.

Go prepared

A paper map or a downloaded guide can help you find your way to a bird watching spot, where it may not be possible to connect to the internet.

Connecting with the community

So much of what we know about bird activity, numbers, and population status is due to a wonderful community of professional and amateur birders, who pool information to add to the general knowledge. As you get more confident in your sightings, you can send in your records to add to that community data bank, often directly via a website or app from a smartphone. One important piece of information is counting birds, which you can also use your phone to help with; either take a quick photo and count from that, or download apps that will help you keep track of your sightings.

Join the flock

If you want to, you can connect with a local group of birders to pool information—and collectively form part of an international community-science effort.

Building your observation skills

Learning to identify birds takes time and patience, and sometimes it might seem as though information just won't lodge in your memory. There are a few strategies that can help with that.

See as well as look

Many people look but don't really *see*, especially if they're just taking photos (similarly, they often hear but don't *listen*). So when you take a photograph, enlarge it and study it, look at the details to familiarize yourself with them. Practice this with birds on your backyard bird feeder. As a starting point, use the observation process on page 44 as a framework to help you learn to work through details such as a bird's shape, markings, and legs systematically. Ultimately, with practice, it will become second nature to observe and evaluate a bird's features.

Write it down

Some people find that writing things down can help their memory. If you're a natural list maker, maybe keep a notebook or spreadsheet to record your observations. Your notes will help train you to look at birds carefully, and because you've written them down yourself, from your own observations, the memory of them may lodge in your brain.

Practice at home
Study the details of the birds that visit your feeder to help you develop your skills of observation.

The more you practice your observation skills, the more intuitive and second nature they'll become

Tap in to your inner artist

Before you reject the idea and insist there is no artist within you, rest assured that you don't really *need* any artistic talent for this approach—honestly. It doesn't really matter if your sketch looks nothing like the bird you are trying to draw; what matters is that you are really *looking* at the bird. You're observing all the details and relative proportions of its head and body shape, length of tail and beak, arrangement of toes, and any distinctive markings or patches of color. The resulting sketch is not the objective: it's the process itself, as that may help you fix details of individual species in your memory.

Does the bird have a "cap" of color on its head or neck?

Are there flashes of color on the wings?

How long are the legs relative to the body?

Keep it basic
Annotate your sketches with the features that stand out for you, to help you learn the bird's key characteristics.

Use a notebook
Making pencil sketches of the birds you see will help you study its features.

About birds

Getting to know birds—
their shapes, their
sounds, their individual
characteristics—
requires neither
expensive equipment
nor even patience,
simply a boundless
curiosity to get under
their feathers.

Put the birds first

Following the birdwatcher's code of conduct will help you avoid the risk of negatively impacting any birds you are watching, by putting their interests first at all times.

Be an ally

Always try to avoid disturbing birds. Follow the rules and laws for visiting the countryside and stay on public paths to avoid disturbing birds' habitat; you could otherwise be causing birds to use up valuable energy they need for feeding, for instance, or perhaps keeping them from their young, who are then left hungry or vulnerable to predation.

Be alert to the signals and behavior of birds, and be careful where you walk. Is a bird making repeated alarm calls, for instance? If it's breeding time, and you're on open ground or a beach, you may be too close to the nest of a ground-nesting bird.

Being still and quiet not only avoids disturbing birds but also means that you'll see more—you won't scare off that wader on a lake shore, or a warbler in a tree, or a finch flock in a field. In close situations, such as a forest, you'll hear most birds before you see them, and they will hear and see you too—so if you're talking as you walk, you'll hear much less, and the birds will move away.

Keep your ears open
In a marsh or forest, you're more likely to hear a bird call than see the bird, so keep quiet and listen.

Casual encounters
Birds in a public park are often used to human company and less likely to be disturbed or agitated by you.

Keep your distance
In open landscapes such as estuaries, watch from a safe distance to avoid disturbing birds, and keep a watch on the tides, too, for your own safety.

Learning to identify birds

Follow this basic framework to help you with rapidly assessing and processing information about a bird you've seen—a process that, with practice, will become second nature.

Getting started

There's no substitute for studying a field guide to get an idea of basic groups of birds (gull, tern, flycatcher, finch, warbler, and so on) and learning the key features of each group. These steps offer a starting point for identifying the birds you see—and the more you become familiar with the general features and geographical spread of individual species, of course, the more you can focus on the critical details and take shortcuts.

1. Context

- Where are you geographically?
- What type of habitat are you in?

Context is key, so these questions will immediately narrow down the range of species you might be looking at.

2. Season

- What time of year is it?

Some species are only present at certain times of year, so that will whittle down your options still further.

3. Visuals

- What size is the bird?
- What sort of beak does the bird have (e.g., length, shape, size, color)?
- What is distinctive about the wing (e.g., length, shape, markings)?
- What is distinctive about the tail (e.g., proportion, length, shape, markings)?

- Is there anything distinctive about the head pattern (e.g., stripes above or through the eye, ring around the eye, or mustache)?

See pages 46–47 for useful terminology to describe them and pages 58–59 for examples of the variations of features.

4. Behavior

- What is the bird doing (e.g., soaring, hopping, walking)?

Some birds have specific patterns of movement or habits that can help you with identification, especially if the light isn't good and you can't see their coloring clearly.

5. Sounds

- What can you hear?

Sometimes it's the call or song that will help you narrow down which species it is and distinguish one bird from another.

Black cap angular, and ragged at rear

Long black bill with pale tip

Black cap rounded

Bill orange with black tip

Black legs

Underside pure white

Short orange legs

Underside pale gray

Sandwich tern

Common tern

What is important?

Learn which features are important to focus on for the kind of bird you are looking at, and the points of difference between similar birds—for example, distinctive beaks, leg colors, and head markings of terns.

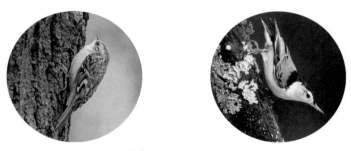

Behavioral pointers

If it's looking up a tree, the bird may be a brown creeper, which climbs upward in a spiral. A white-breasted nuthatch, meanwhile, has a strong grip that permits postures in any direction and often faces downward.

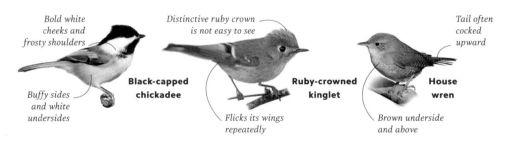

Bold white cheeks and frosty shoulders

Distinctive ruby crown is not easy to see

Tail often cocked upward

Buffy sides and white undersides

Black-capped chickadee

Ruby-crowned kinglet

House wren

Flicks its wings repeatedly

Brown underside and above

Putting the clues together

Colors can help you identify a bird, but against the light, it can seem dark, or pale and bland, so shape, behavior, and calls become more useful. If all you have is a silhouette, calls and song may be of help.

Anatomy of a bird

Although birds vary hugely from species to species in aspects such as plumage and size, the basic anatomy is luckily very similar, and learning the terminology will help you identify birds.

What's what on a bird

Birders use precise terminology, describing the parts of a bird very specifically to map its markings and coloration in as much detail as possible.

Understanding basic bird anatomy will also give you a huge appreciation for how perfectly birds are built for flight: their lightweight beak instead of heavy teeth and jawbones; their lightweight yet strong skeleton; their streamlined shape and surfaces—even their legs can be tucked away to reduce drag in flight. Some birds are capable of high-speed aerobatics in short bursts, such as swallows and falcons; others are supremely efficient endurance fliers such as godwits, which can remain airborne for days at a time, and swifts, which live on the wing for months on end.

Scapulars

Tertiaries

Primaries

Tail

Under tail coverts

Vent

Hollow bones are honeycombed for lightness combined with rigidity

Hind claw

Engineered for flight

Most of a bird's bones are hollow, to reduce body weight. Thanks to the bones' honeycomb structure, however, the skeleton is very strong. The feathers are made from the same material as human hair and nails—keratin—and different types of feathers perform specific functions.

Map of a bird
Learning these terms helps you look at a bird, such as this blue jay, in more detail, and share information with other birders more easily.

Eye markings, such as eyebrow or eyestripe

Crown or cap

Cheek

Lore

Nape

Bill

Back

Throat

Primary coverts

Secondary coverts

Breast

Secondary coverts

Upper tail coverts

Primary coverts

Rump

Flank

Scapulars

Belly

Thigh

Leg

Tertiaries

Toe

Secondaries

Primaries

On the wing
Wing feathers are designed to generate thrust and lift with precise control.

A gallery of feathers

While you may not be able to get near to birds, many birds shed feathers that you can inspect close-up. The gallery opposite (not to scale) shows their beauty and variety. There are different types of feathers, each performing different functions, including sensory, insulating, and aerodynamic. The function of covert feathers, for example, is to smooth the airflow over the wings and tail; they cover the base of the different types of wing and tail feathers and are named accordingly (*see p. 47*).

Which type of feather is it?

The structure, shape, and color of a feather will reveal not just which bird it belonged to but where on the bird's body it came from and what its function was.

Tail feathers have a central shaft and are for steering, balance, and display

Wing feathers have a shaft off-center and are shaped to provide power for flight

Bristles may detect prey by touch or help catch flies in the bill

Contour feathers smooth air flow over the wing and waterproof the head and body

Semiplume feathers are weak and downy, adding insulation

Down feathers lie next to the skin and insulate a bird's body

Filoplumes are sensory feathers, but their exact function is not known

Blue feathers are actually very rare in nature—almost all blue feathers are a result of structural color

Untrue blue

Strange as it may seem, in nature there are almost no blue feathers; they appear blue because of the way the light is reflected from them, not due to pigmentation.

Belted Kingfisher feather

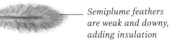

Light bouncing off the surface of the dull, brown feather creates blues and greens

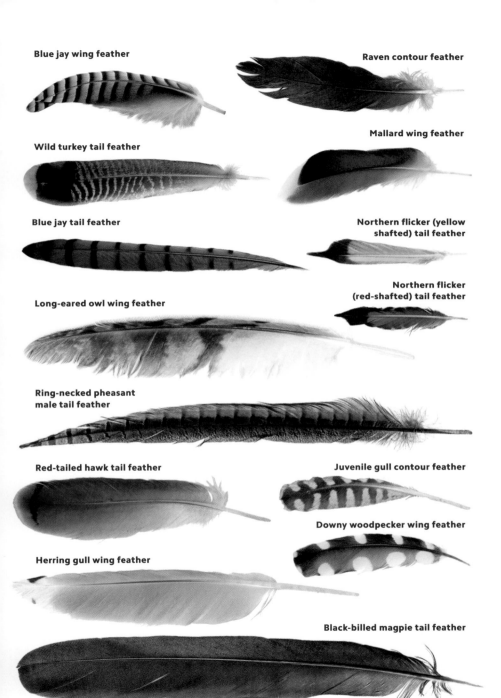

Blue jay wing feather

Raven contour feather

Wild turkey tail feather

Mallard wing feather

Blue jay tail feather

Northern flicker (yellow shafted) tail feather

Northern flicker (red-shafted) tail feather

Long-eared owl wing feather

Ring-necked pheasant male tail feather

Red-tailed hawk tail feather

Juvenile gull contour feather

Downy woodpecker wing feather

Herring gull wing feather

Black-billed magpie tail feather

Colors and markings

Bird life offers a wonderful variety of color and pattern—
often even within a species. A bird's plumage may be dictated
by many factors, such as diet, breeding, and age.

Why are birds the colors they are?

Many birds are not brightly colored (such as the "LBJs"—the "little brown jobs"), as they
want to stay as inconspicuous as possible. In species where competition for mates is
strong, the males are generally striking and colorful—at least during the breeding
season—while females' plumage is more camouflaged. In a few species, this is reversed:
in breeding season, red phalaropes are bright while the males are dull. Where species
have long-lasting pair bonds, such as tundra swans, there is little difference between
the sexes. Plumage may change as the bird matures, with the seasons, or for breeding.

Designed to impress
While the male green-winged
teal has colorful plumage to
woo a mate, the female's
plainer streaked brown
plumage keeps her safely
camouflaged on the nest.

Clever camouflage

Some birds, such as this juvenile winter wren, use color to blend with their surroundings and hide from predators. Birds such as ptarmigan even change color with the seasons.

A warning sign

The red feathers of the fiercely territorial red-winged blackbird are a stark warning, to deter others from encroaching on its territory before resorting to fighting.

Why birds change their appearance

Just when you think you have started to recognize some species, they change their plumage, so you have yet more learning to do—but there's always a reason for those changes.

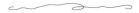

Making changes

There are many reasons why birds might change their plumage: often as part of a molt, when old, faded, worn, and torn feathers are replaced with new ones ready for the year ahead; sometimes as part of maturing from juvenile to adult bird; to help with seasonal camouflaging; and in preparation for courtship, when fresh, colorful plumage can help attract a mate.

Learning all these extra variations can seem daunting. But these changes don't happen overnight, so you'll see a lot of "in-between" transitional patterns too that can help you make the connections. And, while some groups, like gulls, go through many changes, others remain reassuringly consistent. The reward for noticing these changes, though, is an insight into what's happening in the bird's life at that moment.

Blending in
Many species have a duller plumage in winter, but ptarmigan become pure white to camouflage them against the snow.

Cap and bill are
olive brown

Throat is
yellow and
breast is brown

Black cap
appears in spring

Bill turns
orange

Winter American goldfinch
The male American goldfinch
has dull plumage in winter—a
striking change from its bright
summer colors.

Summer American goldfinch
In spring, the dull winter body feathers
are quickly replaced by brilliant
canary-yellow feathers, while the
wing feathers remain jet black.

Changing with the seasons

Although the plumage colors of some birds, such as
American robins, are relatively constant, the adult birds
of other species change their plumage with the seasons.
This is to make sure that they look their best for
the breeding season, before reverting to their
nonbreeding plumage again. For most birds, such
as warblers, finches, tanagers, and waders, this means
dull winter colors, but much brighter hues in summer,
with even the bill color changing in many species.

For others, the pattern of change is slightly different:
ducks, for instance, look their "best" in winter, when
they pair up during the courtship phase, and males
actually have their dullest plumage in summer. As
ground nesters, meanwhile, female ducks don't need
bright colors, which could attract predators, so
their dull plumage helps camouflage them on the nest.

All at once
Male mallards molt their wing
feathers all at once, becoming
flightless for a while. During this
process, the male's plumage is
similar to the female's—apart
from the telltale yellow bill.

Signs of growing up

Depending on the species, a chick goes through a sequence of molts (replacing feathers) before adopting its adult plumage. For small birds, this may take the pattern of a rapid fall molt (usually only partial) to produce a first-winter plumage, then in spring another change into their adult plumage. For larger birds, the spring change may produce their adult plumage, or it may be only the first in a series of different plumages over a few years.

Juvenile plumage

Steps to maturity

Some large birds, such as gulls, may have second-, third-, even fourth-year plumages as they gradually mature into their adult plumage. As shown here, a herring gull goes through several years of plumage change.

Tan-brown with checkerboard patterning above, very dark eyes, and a dark bill

First-winter plumage

Pale pink base and tip on the bill, and grayer body feathers appearing above, but the eyes remain dark

The back shows more gray feathers

Juvenile feathers on wings and tail are faded and paler

The underparts are whiter, and the eyes are paler

Second-winter plumage

Nonbreeding adult

Extensive streaking on the neck, and the eyes are pale

The head is white from February to August, streaked at other times

During molt, worn, browner feathers are replaced by new black and white ones

The bill is now yellow with a red patch, and the eye is yellow

Fourth-year gulls are white below and clear gray above

Breeding adult

The underparts are a cleaner white

More gray on the back and wings

Third-winter plumage

Preening
and maintenance

When they're not feeding, birds are often engaged in the essential task of preening, as feathers need to be kept in tip-top condition for flight and for weatherproofing against the elements.

Preening

Birds preen their feathers to keep them free of parasites and dirt, moisturize them with an oil they produce naturally (called preen oil) so that they stay flexible and strong, and align them in optimum position for waterproofing and flight.

In addition to preening, various other techniques are used to maintain feathers: stretching out the wings or fluffing the feathers; sunbathing; and also bathing in water, dust, or even ants (it's thought birds rub formic acid from the ants' bodies on their feathers to repel parasites).

Realigning feathers
This belted kingfisher is using its bill to adjust its wing feathers so that they are perfectly aligned for efficient flight.

Molting

Most birds molt each year, replacing old, worn-out feathers with new, strong ones ready for winter—and for the breeding season. Juveniles molt to grow their adult plumage. Molting takes lots of energy and can leave a bird flightless and vulnerable, so timing is key. For example, a female raptor will start to molt while incubating her eggs; a male can delay molting until the chicks have fledged and can feed themselves. Ducks are flightless when molting in summer, before they need to migrate.

Having a dust bath
Many birds, including this female bobwhite, use regular dust baths to dislodge parasites and absorb any excess preen oil they might have produced.

Bathing in water
Songbirds such as this
female Northern cardinal
will first wash off dirt and
parasites before preening
their feathers back
into alignment.

Shaped for a purpose

In nature, form is always determined by function. Factors such as flying habits, feeding, habitat, and migration have led to a myriad of evolutionary adaptations—some highly specialized.

Wings and flight

A bird's flight action may be linked to its wing shape, but sometimes only loosely. Broad, bowed wings give a great blue heron stability, and crescent-shaped wings help a swift dash across the sky. Warblers flit through foliage on small, round wings yet migrate across whole continents. Fingered wing tips help large birds of prey soar, while pointed wings give falcons extra speed—yet a kestrel can also hover as if suspended on a string.

Catching the wind
A gannet glides on the wind; its long wings and small flight muscles make that harder in calm air.

Soaring
Broad, fingered wings help vultures soar high up before gliding into the distance.

Life in the air
Scythe-like wings help swifts live on the wing, chasing after insect prey.

Getting around
Crows have an "all-purpose" elliptical wing shape for steady flight.

Bills and feeding

The shape of a bird's bill can be related to its feeding habits. Birds such as thrushes might have an "all-purpose" straight bill for eating berries, probing for worms, and catching insects. Others are more specialized: the heron's dagger bill for snatching fish, for example, or the merganser's serrated beak for gripping fish. Here are a few of the many different specialist beak shapes that have evolved.

Filter-feeding
Waterbirds such as mallards use their beaks to filter food from mud and water.

Drilling
A woodpecker's beak can chisel a nest hole in a tree and probe into bark for food.

Feet and toes

Most land birds have three toes pointing forward and one pointing backward, but owls and woodpeckers have the outer toe turned back for a wider grip, and some waders have no hind toe at all. Perching birds' toes are curled into a firm grip. Webbed feet push ducks and swans through water, but lobed toes do the same for coots and grebes.

Swimming
Webbed toes spread wide to push down and against the water on the back stroke then fold together to slip through on the front stroke.

Climbing
Sharp claws help many birds grip bark but in woodpeckers the long third toe also points backward, giving it extra gripping power.

Catching
Curved, razorlike claws help birds of prey catch and carry their prey; this owl kills its prey with its sharp claws.

Perching
A short hind toe curls around the perch, allowing perching birds such as this crow to grip onto a branch.

Wading
Long toes allow birds such as this egret to walk over mud and give extra support when the bird leans far forward.

Walking
Small walking birds, such as horned larks and pipits, have a long hind claw that helps with stability.

Ripping flesh
Birds of prey have a hooked bill to tear flesh; falcons have a killing bite.

Cracking seeds
A wide tongue and thick, strong bill helps the evening gosbeak to manipulate seeds.

Catching insects
Bristles and a wide base to the bill help insect-feeders such as this flycatcher snap up flies.

Probing
A curlew's long bill allows it to penetrate into silt or mud to catch small crabs.

How bird senses work

Birds have the same five senses as us, albeit with adaptations and, in many cases, enhancements compared to our own senses. They also have other enhanced "senses," such as spatial awareness and a sense of direction for navigation.

Sight and sound

A bird's eyes have more cells that capture information and carry it to the brain than we do, giving them a wider range of vision. For example, they can see colors in the ultraviolet range, which we are unable to do, and the eyes of night-hunters, such as owls, are more sensitive than ours to low light. Some species have amazing visual abilities: for example, starlings can focus inside the tip of their open beak as they probe for food, while simultaneously watching the horizon for danger.

You'll often see a bird looking alert, as if watching for predators or looking for food, but usually it's also listening. Calls and songs play a vital part in birds' lives, so their hearing is excellent. In owls, the ears are located behind a disc of stiff feathers, with one ear larger or lower than the other. The minute difference in the timing of sound reaching each ear helps them pinpoint the exact position of the prey making a faint rustle in vegetation.

Wired for sound

The heart-shaped face of a barn owl acts to trap and focus sound, and a large part of its brain is dedicated to processing noises.

Touch

Some birds find their food by touch: a snipe probing the mud for worms with a bill-tip full of nerve endings, for example, or an avocet sweeping its bill through water to "feel" for food. Woodcocks use their beaks to sense the movement of worms in the soil. Sensitive bristles around the bill may help insect-eating birds catch prey in flight, and even feathers let some birds detect the movement of the air as they fly.

Smell and taste

For many birds, smell and taste are not highly developed senses, although studies are revealing that they have greater importance than was once thought. Birds have relatively few taste buds compared to mammals, but sweet sugary tastes may draw them to valuable food such as berries.

Spatial awareness

Some birds, such as starlings and knots, form flocks that can perform highly synchronized aerial maneuvers, but how do they not collide? How do they know when to swerve and dive? Their spatial awareness is thought to allow each bird to track just the birds around itself, filtering out the rest of the flock.

Similarly, how do birds such as swifts and swallows fly rapidly without hitting anything? It's because their brain can categorize and filter out nonessential visual information to focus on speed and distance.

On the tip of the tongue
The sticky tip of a Northern flicker's extra-long tongue can catch larvae hidden under tree bark or inside a tree cavity.

Starling aerobatics
Birds use optic flow—the apparent motion of static objects while moving—to help them adjust their speed and spacing.

Identifying a bird in flight

Being able to identify a bird in flight—at a distance, or while moving quickly, or in the sun's glare—is not easy, but learning to recognize flight actions, and wing and tail shapes, helps narrow down the options.

Distinctive flight patterns

Watch how a bird flies: some fly straight and even; others undulate up and down; large soaring birds save energy by rising in circles and then gliding. You can get clues, too, from how a bird flocks: crows form busy, irregular flocks; gulls often fly in lines and Vs; cranes and geese may form Vs or chevrons, although some fly in random groups. Goldfinches fly in loose groups, but house sparrows and house finches form tighter flocks; siskins and crossbills fly in close, synchronized groups, while grosbeaks do so in ones and twos. Ravens may soar, but crows usually flap. Teach yourself to take note of a bird's flight pattern, flocking habit, and wing action.

Direct
Herons and other waterfowl tend to fly in straight lines.

Undulating
Most woodpeckers have deep undulations; Goldfinches and chickadees may bob and dart more, especially the chickadees.

Flap-and-glide
Birds as varied as shearwaters, swallows, and accipiters have bursts of flaps between glides.

Erratic
Owls tend to flutter and change direction, flying relatively erratically and slowly.

Soaring
Eagles, buteos, and vultures gain height using thermals to soar without wingbeats, then move off in a long, straight glide.

Shape and markings
The large size and long, slightly upturned bill suggest godwits. The overall buffy color and cinnamon wing linings confirm these are marbled godwits.

A characteristic shape

In combination, the shape of the wing and the tail—and whether during flight the head and neck are long or short, withdrawn, or extended—may combine to create distinctive silhouettes in flight, both for herons, cranes, and other large birds, and for smaller birds such as swifts and swallows.

Birds of prey can generally be grouped into pointed-winged species (falcons) and broad-winged birds (such as buteos); and into those that hold their wings flat during flight and those that soar with their wings raised (such as turkey vultures). Not all large soaring birds are birds of prey, however. You'll also see ravens and even gulls circling high up, too, and American white pelicans will ride the thermals during migration. Tails may be pointed, rounded, shallowly or deeply forked, squared, or fan-shaped. In flight, birds use their tails as rudders for precise steering and changes of height. Many birds have similar flight patterns despite different tail shapes, however, so it is ultimately a question of watching, thinking about what you see, and learning.

At great height, or with birds flying quickly, it's hard to see markings or even overall color, so combining overall shape and flight style and pattern will give you a good starting point to narrow down the options.

Which birds flock, and why?

Some birds are seldom seen alone, others are rarely if ever in flocks other than family groups, and some seem happy with either. It can be fascinating to watch a flock foraging—perhaps on a field or on the water—or see one performing its amazing aerial maneuvers.

Foraging benefits

Some birds group together in nesting colonies to be safe from predators, but for other birds flocking often has to do with food: many eyes are better than one at finding food that is widely but thinly scattered. Many woodland birds stay territorial in summer, when they are nesting and food is plentiful, but flock together afterward. Some form mixed flocks, with chickadees and titmice, and even woodpeckers coming together; the benefits can include less competition for particular foods that each species prefer. There is much variation, though: in some places, house sparrows breed in colonies where food is abundant, and while species such as eiders and scoters feed in flocks, other waterfowl don't, and cormorants seem happy to do either.

Protection and migration

Many eyes are also better at spotting a predator approaching, whether on the ground or up in the air, although some species, such as wrens, prefer to stay solitary, relying on camouflage and hiding.

Entirely black and glossy, crows are often seen in groups

Although many birds migrate alone or in small groups, some species, such as swallows, migrate in large numbers, but usually widely spread. Juveniles will often innately know in which direction to fly. Others, such as swans and cranes migrate in flocks with adults to learn how far to go; however, many don't—sandpipers, for example, migrate entirely alone. It's always worth looking at flocks of waterfowl, geese, and shorebirds in case you see an unexpected fellow traveler—migrant groups and wintering flocks can attract other birds that get "caught up" in the crowd and appear in unexpected places.

Social birds

Crows are highly intelligent and social birds. They usually sleep in large roosts where they are safer from owls, and, scientist believe, they may exchange information about where to find food.

Safety in numbers
As a peregrine falcon dives into the flock, the starlings swoop away and regroup. With so many targets for the falcon, the risk for each individual starling is minimized.

Roosting together

Research suggests that American crows usually roost together at night for better protection from great horned owls. Some crow roosts can be as big as about two million individuals.

All the same way

Black skimmers also roost in groups where they are safer from predators. They usually all face the same direction, into the wind, to reduce the loss of body heat.

Why birds roost

When birds sleep—alone or in flocks—they "roost." A sleeping flock may be called a roost, as may be the place where they are sleeping. Roosting offers security, warmth, and sometimes communication.

Warmth and safety

After a long day feeding, rearing a brood, or migrating, roosting allows birds to recuperate and keep their plumage in good condition. Roosting together at night (or in coastal areas at high tide, when many birds' feeding grounds are underwater) offers the security of multiple pairs of eyes, so some birds flock at night even if they feed alone by day. Roosting as a flock also lets large numbers of birds share suitable spaces, which are often over water (such as red-winged blackbirds in a marsh), or up high (crows in treetops, for example). For small birds that must spend all day feeding to store energy, roosting in groups offers shared body heat that helps them save energy and stay warm on a cold night.

Perks of age

At large roosts, such as woodland sites, older birds may get the best places in the middle, which are warmest and least likely to be predated. Young birds are pushed out to the colder edges, more vulnerable to predators—and more likely to get covered in other birds' droppings! Experts think roosting crows may share information on good feeding sites, or they may simply follow the best-fed birds the next morning.

Solitary roost
After hunting by night, an eastern screech-owl may roost tucked in a tree hole or up in an evergreen tree; white droppings below may give you a clue.

While roosting, crows seem to share information with each other on good sites for the next day's feeding

Giveaway calls
Hidden in the cattail stems, the marsh wren may stay out of sight, but you might hear its rhythmic, repetitive, churring song.

Calls, songs, and sounds

Very often, the clue to a bird's presence is not a glimpse of it but a sound. You may hear a bird long before you catch sight of it. As well as calls and songs, some birds have other, particular noises that help us track them.

Not just calls

You might think birds just sing or call, but there are actually far more sounds in their repertoire, such as drumming, booming, and wing-clapping. In dense vegetation, such as marshes or forests, listen carefully and you may hear birds you can't yet see, such as the pumping of an American bittern in search of a female to mate with in the marsh, or the quiet crack of crossbills opening pine cones, and the thud of discarded cones falling to the ground.

Pigeons do not call in flight, but pigeons and doves frequently communicate by making a loud "clap" with their wings, which is especially obvious with rock pigeons. Short-eared owls also clap their wings. Tundra swans can make a whistling sound with their wings, which is why they are sometimes called "whistling" swans. Mute swans make a musical, throbbing hum with their wings that can be heard a long way off.

Headbangers

There are strange noises to be heard within the woods. All the functions of a song are replaced by a nonvocal sound when a pileated woodpecker "drums." It rapidly vibrates its bill against a branch (or telephone pole, if the pole makes the right noise) creating an abrupt sound that carries far through the trees.

The winnowing of snipe

When a Wilson's snipe dives as part of its courtship display, its outspread stiff outer tail feathers vibrate to create a "winnowing" sound.

Why birds sing and call

If birdsong betrays their presence, why do some species make so much noise? How can some birds keep singing so loudly for so long? And what's the difference between a call and a song?

What are they communicating?

In general, birds sing for two reasons: to attract a mate ("listen to me, I'm clever, I'm strong"); and to defend territory ("this spot is mine, keep away"). Birds also use "contact calls" to keep in touch as they forage or in flight; these often sound similar within related groups. Thanks to a special organ called a syrinx, birds can trill and sing two notes at the same time. Some, such as the winter wren, can maintain a constant output of song too. And while some birds seem to learn songs or calls in the egg, others learn songs as fledglings. Young birds can pick up a regional "accent" from their parents (a cardinal in the north will sound different from one in the south, for example), and some birds even learn to mimic other birds or sounds (such as a cellphone ringtone).

Song or call?

During the day—particularly at dawn—musical songs are sung by many species, often by the males. Calls are shorter and more functional, such as contact calls, alarm calls, and juvenile calls for food. Hidden in his habitat, a male bird eager to mate needs to let females know, so often the denser the vegetation, the louder or more penetrating the calls (such as a bittern booming in the cattails). Warning calls are often thin and hard to pinpoint, while alarm calls may be sharp or "harder" to clearly communicate a bird's position.

Ready for more
Hungry young starlings call to tell their parents to signal that they're ready for more food.

Song in flight
As a ground-nesting bird, the horned lark sings its song from the sky or fence posts near suitable open sites.

Sound and vision
To reinforcing his rhythmic song, a male golden-crowned kinglet might also fan his yellow crest.

A mighty cascade
Despite its diminutive stature, the winter wren sings loudly, frequently, and intensely, releasing a stream of high notes interspersed with trills.

Learning songs and calls

Wouldn't it be wonderful to be able to recognize the calls of different birds? You can use an app as a shortcut, but there's no substitute for putting in the work to memorize them for yourself. It takes time to learn the language of birds, however, so be patient.

Listen and look

By far the best way to memorize a bird's call is to see it at the same time so that the call sticks in your brain. It is easy to use an app on your phone or listen to recordings online, but they won't help you memorize sound and identity together.

So just as you should not just see but really *look*, so also you should not just hear but really *listen*. Describe the call or song in a contextual way to help fix it in your memory: the evening call of a whip-poor-will from the woods, the song of a horned lark over farm fields, or the "yodeling" of a male common loon to proclaim his territory.

Log them down

If it helps you to remember calls and songs, write them down. Make up your own words that capture the sound for you, or use descriptive terms such as churring, trilling, buzzing, liquid, slurred, sharp, shouted; they'll help you get a grip on the "quality" of a sound. Use question marks and exclamations. Write down the pattern or form—"chwee," "chip," "chirreee," or whatever—and don't worry if you need to use a bit of artistic license (such as the call "cu-ckoo," which may really be nearer to "u-oo," but that doesn't quite convey the right sound).

That's not to say you shouldn't use an app; apps can help you isolate and connect with what you're listening to and log what you're hearing so you can replay the call later. But if you take the time to learn the songs and calls, it's like being able to understand a language rather than just getting your phone to translate everything for you.

The bigger picture

Like the call of this meadow lark, which can be heard over farms in summer, so many bird sounds are linked to a place, a time, or a season that may help you to memorize them.

Getting started

Here are five relatively unique songs that you could use for initial identification "practice." Commonly found in many parks and gardens, these birds have distinctive calls that are reasonably easy to learn. Try to watch the birds as they are singing, too, to help "fix" the song in your memory.

Tufted titmouse
The high "peter peter" song of the tufted titmouse has great carrying power through the forest.

American robin
Clear and melodic, with warbles and whistles, this bird sings "cheerily-cheerup, cheerup, cheerily-cheerup."

Hermit thrush
The ethereal, flutelike song of the hermit thrush typically ends with a higher-pitched, questioning note.

Rose-breasted grosbeak
A treetop singer, the rose-breasted grosbeak has a musical song with sharp squeaks and without pauses.

Red-winged blackbird
The male red-winged blackbird's song sounds like "conk-la-ree." Females make a series of "chit" sounds.

Using an app

There are many apps that can identify birdsongs with varying degrees of accuracy. Choose one that is specific to your geographical location. Make sure your phone is fully charged if you're going to rely on it to identify bird calls, and ideally carry a power pack for recharging.

A birdsong app can help you identify which birds are nearby, so you know what to look out for

Finding a mate

There are two main strategies birds use for courtship: visual display and acoustic performance. They have varied, colorful, and sometimes spectacular techniques to woo a mate.

Visual displays

Males usually do the courting, and their displays have two main functions: to impress watching females (or to reinforce existing pair bonds) and to deter rival males. In many species, males have more colorful plumage than females, which they use to attract the attention of mates, sometimes with sounds and actions too. Males' plumage needs to be in tip-top condition to convince females that they are the strongest suitor. For example, the brightness and contrast of the male black-capped chickadee's plumage can serve as a signal to potential mates about the male's health. Some bird species have specific courtship plumage, such as the tail feathers of the wild turkey, the long tail of a male pheasant, and the crest of a male cardinal.

For some, courtship is a communal activity, for example, the "lek" of the prairie chicken, which involves multiple males and females. Solitary suitors include meadowlarks, horned larks, and pipits, who deploy a delicate song-flight to woo their mate. Often a mixture of both action and sound, courtship can be complex, such as

Spectacular flights
Male ruby-throated hummingbirds perform fantastic courtship flights with their wings humming to attract the females.

Parachute display
A male horned lark sings in courtship as it rises vertically, then "parachutes" down with its wings folded and tail lifted.

Shake a tail feather
Within groups called "leks," male prairie chickens fan out their tail feathers, strike a pose, and make bubbling sounds to attract females.

the reciprocal displays by pairs of western grebes, and over time pairs that mate for life can "personalize" their rituals.

Serenading with song
As part of their courtship strategy, some species rely on calls, song, and other sounds, such as cooing or "clapping" their wings.

Birds such as thrushes will sing from a perch, while others such as the horned lark sing in flight. Some males stick to a script characteristic of the species, but others might use mimicry and phrases learned from other males or even other species. In some species, there are even regional "dialects" in songs and calls.

Competitive display
Male goldeneye ducks compete for the attention of females by performing a communal display of calls and maneuvers on the water.

Nests and nest sites

The "classic" cup of twigs in a tree is just one of a great variety of styles, shapes, and sites different birds use for their nests, from basic scrapes on the ground to intricate feats of engineering.

Builders and renters

Nests are not birds' homes, they are simply where they lay eggs and often, raise their chicks. But some birds exert a lot more effort than others over the building process—from the few gathered stones on a gravel parking lot for a killdeer nest to the blue-gray gnatcatcher's lichen-covered nest woven together with spider webs. And while buteos, accipiters, and kites make their own stick nests, falcons will just use old crows' nests or simply lay eggs on ledges with a bit of soft lining. Hole-nesters such as chickadees and titmice will use existing holes, but woodpeckers usually make their own. You may easily spot the massive stick nests of ospreys and eagles.

Location, location

Different species have their own strategies to keep their eggs safe. Many nests are up in trees or on ledges, but those made by kingfishers and bank swallows are hidden in banks and roots, and Carolina wrens may nest in tree cavities and stumps. Grebe nests may float; coot nests are built up from the bottom in shallow water. Some birds nest in colonies, perhaps high in trees or out on rocky islets. If you see birds flitting around a hedge, or calling insistently, you may be close to a nest. Whatever you do, avoid disturbing them, as this may cause them to abandon the nest, or you may alert a predator to its presence.

Under the eaves
Cliff swallows build their mud nests under building eaves and bridges.

On the ground
The eggs of a killdeer are camouflaged amidst the surrounding pebbles.

On a rocky ledge
A common murre will lay its egg on just a bare rock ledge.

In a tree
The soft, warm nest of a tufted titmouse is lined with fur from racoons, dogs, cats, and mice, and sometimes human hair.

Raising a family

There are many variations on how many eggs a female lays, what color they are, and what happens after hatching. Where the nest is placed plays a part in what occurs next, too.

Clutches and broods

A "clutch" is a batch of eggs, which hatch to become a "brood" of chicks. Eggs are laid with myriad patterns: hole-nesting species may have white eggs that they can see in the dark; others eggs may be camouflaged (blackbird) or even sky-blue (American robin).

Seabirds may lay one or two eggs, while golden-crowned kinglets, for example, lay up to 11 eggs. Some birds rear only one brood per season; others up to three. Sometimes a single large brood will coincide with an abundance of food; other birds produce smaller broods over the summer with a less plentiful supply of food. Even similar species may have different strategies: barred owls nest in the same territory for years, laying few eggs, while short-eared owls go wherever the food is, laying more eggs in some years but none in others.

Ready for action—or not

Some chicks, such as those of ground-nesting species, are "precocial," meaning they hatch pretty much ready to be mobile and feed for themselves. Other chicks are "altricial," staying in the nest until they develop feathers and "fledge" (take their first flight). Vulnerable to predators and reliant on their parents for their food supply, the chicks may even become heavier than their parents as they build up energy reserves for their first flight.

Ready to fledge
Well-developed within the egg, the chicks of the mute swan hatch ready to swim and feed, although they cannot fly for about five months.

When timing is key
Carolina chickadees often nest near native trees that are known to house large numbers of caterpillars. Parents must bring home more than 350 caterpillars per day to raise one brood.

Finding food

Foraging for food takes up a huge part of many birds' daily lives, and different species have developed their own techniques, from physical adaptations to behavioral strategies. Habitat decline and climate change add to the challenges they face.

The need to feed

Few birds can fast for long. Small ones in particular must feed constantly to stay alive, especially when preparing for a long migration, or during the cold days and long nights of winter, when keeping warm uses up a lot of energy.

While some birds flock together to maximize their chances of finding food, some species have evolved to become specialist feeders, such as the yellow-bellied sapsucker, which has a bushy-tipped tongue that it uses to extract sap from trees, or the serrated edges of a merganser's bill, which is ideal for holding onto a wriggling fish. Other birds use techniques rather than adaptations: herring gulls will drop shellfish onto rocks to break them open, for example, while green herons use scavenged bread to bait fish close enough to strike. Species such as nuthatches and jays even store food for later, while others simply steal: laughing gulls will steal food from terns to feed to their own chicks.

Clever strategies
The oystercatcher can hammer shells open or slide its bill between the two halves to pry them apart.

Evolved adaptations
The tweezer-like beak of a crossbill is ideal for extracting the seeds inside pine cones.

Habitat is key

Access to unpolluted habitat is vital. Grebes and herons, kingfishers and mergansers, kittiwakes and terns all need clean, healthy water for their fish prey to thrive, so pollution can spell disaster. Likewise, estuarine birds need rich foraging habitats of wet mud, washed and refreshed by unpolluted tidal waters. Pollution, sea-warming, and over-fishing all present threats to bird populations.

Farmland once provided much more food for many birds, but intensive farming practices have caused, for example, the loss of meadows on which owls and kestrels once hunted for prey; of safe nesting sites for harriers; and of stubble fields once alive with huge mixed flocks of horned larks, snow buntings, and pipits. Pesticide use has drastically impacted the insect food needed by swallows, warblers, and so many other birds. Gulls still "follow the plow," seeking worms and other food turned up with the cultivated soil. Regenerative and other wildlife-friendly farming practices may help birds in the future.

Feeding as a flock
Where food is temporarily plentiful, flocking birds such as red-winged blackbirds, grackles, and cowbirds may forage together.

The importance of margins
Habitats managed for birds may look "messy" but they provide good cover from predators, shelter, and food such as sunflower seeds.

Moving on mass
Swarms of red knots spend the winter in coastal regions as far south as South America, having migrated from their breeding grounds in the Arctic.

Where do they go?

Bird migration has long been one of the great mysteries of the natural world: three-fourths of North American species migrate each year, but how do they know where and when to go?

Incredible journeys

Migration is chiefly a means of maximizing birds' exploitation of available food and nesting areas—but that doesn't do justice to the remarkable or even epic flights that this can sometimes involve—the navigation skills, endurance, and dangers.

Imagine yourself as an adolescent, without education, maps, signposts, books, TV, or the internet. One day, you have such an irresistible urge to go that you start to head off to South America—how do you even know there is such a place, let alone where it might be? Nevertheless, off you go, to spend a winter in South America, before returning unaided back to your garden. You have just replicated the actions of a cuckoo, barn swallow, cerulean warbler, or broad-winged hawk. These birds, wonderfully, return to the very same tree or shed where they bred the year before, or where they were reared.

As juveniles, some birds, such as ospreys and common terns, fly to South America but do not return for a couple of years, when they are old enough to breed. Waders may navigate the whole of the Arctic and subarctic regions, flying huge distances from the far north to stop over at specific beaches and estuaries just as they did in past years, and their ancestors did before them. Tundra swans and brant fly in from Alaska every fall and return there in spring. Some seabirds spend the winter at sea, often with an eyeline just above the waves, but return unerringly to their native cliffs and islands.

Masters of navigation

Some species fly directly; others take winding routes along landmarks. Some fly out and back along the same route; others have a more circular journey. Some stop and feed along the way; others tackle the whole journey in one nonstop flight. Over short distances, landmarks can be used, but more often birds rely on detecting magnetic fields, using special cells in their eyes, or navigating by the sun and stars. Young geese, swans, and cranes learn migration routes from their parents, but young shorebirds, osprey, and most young landbirds instinctively know where to migrate.

But how do they know which direction to go, when, and how far to fly? Much of the information about direction and distance of flight is, incredibly, encoded in their genes, and an internal clock lets them know when it's time to migrate. They also learn from experience, so their first migration is always the most perilous.

Tell-tale clues

It's easy to develop a keen eye for giveaway signs of bird activity, even if the birds themselves are out of sight. With a bit of detective work, you can still establish which birds are active around you.

Signs of habitation

Seeing a nest is not always about looking up into a tree; it may be twigs on a ledge, for example, or holes tunneled into a sand bank. Bird poop—on the ground or on rafters—is a sign of roosting activity.

Often the clues are on the ground, so remember to look down as well as up

The poop is actually the black stuff; the white is the urine (it's not very watery because birds tend to conserve water to help guard against dehydration). Similarly, you might see pellets regurgitated by birds on the ground. Pellets contain all the undigested parts of their food, such as fur, bones, scales, feathers, or even just seed husks. Many birds make pellets, but you're mostly likely to spot those made by owls and raptors, or maybe those of a kingfisher or heron.

Other signs of birds feeding might include, for example, holes drilled in a tree trunk by a woodpecker, or hazelnuts jammed into a bark crevice—a possible sign that a woodpecker or nuthatch has been trying to hammer the nuts open.

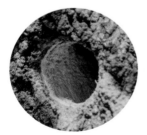

Cavities in tree bark
Look for hollows made by woodpeckers, which are used for nesting.

Burrows in a bank
Bank swallows make their nests in holes burrowed into a sandy bank by a shoreline.

Pellets on the ground
Owls and other birds drop regurgitated pellets, revealing traces of their latest meal.

Signs of other activity

Scattered feathers in a cavity or on the ground may be from a bird molting nearby or, particularly if they are the fluffy inner layer of down feathers, a recent kill on a predator's plucking post. You may spot egg fragments on the ground, too, but these are not always signs of a nearby nest, as parents may drop hatched eggshells away from the nest to divert attention, or the egg may have been predated. You may even be able

Ghostly sign
Glass is confusing for birds, and many fly into windows—sometimes fatally. Impacting at full speed, as this pigeon did, leaves a clear imprint on the glass.

to figure out whether it was taken by a predator: an egg that hatches naturally when a chick emerges usually breaks in half quite cleanly; on predated eggs, the breaks are likely to be more irregular.

Holes in trees
Pileated woodpeckers excavate rectangular feeding holes; within lie insect meals.

Pine cone husks
A pine cone stripped clean of its seeds betrays the activity of an efficient crossbill.

Fragments of eggshell
Bits of shell suggest a hatched chick is nearby—or, in this case, that a predator ate it.

Bringing birds
to you

Often you have to
go to the birds, but
sometimes you can
encourage them to come
to you—and when
they do, you will find
that there's nothing
better than sharing your
space with a wild
creature.

Creating a
bird-friendly space

There are many ways to make your outdoor space as attractive as possible for birds—and even a small terrace, balcony, or window box can support bird activity.

Providing for their needs

Birds need food, water, a place to roost, and somewhere to nest. If you can provide any or all of these elements, then you can attract birds into your outdoor space. Besides hanging bird feeders in strategic positions, think carefully about what you choose to plant. The flowers and plants you grow can entice insects on which birds can feed, and later in the year they may produce seeds or berries for birds to eat in fall and winter.

Feeding station
Flowering tree blossoms attract insects, which in turn draw birds such as this purple finch. Orioles and some warblers also feed on these insects.

If you have space for native shrubs, and provide hedges rather than fences, you're offering places to nest, which you can also supplement with nest boxes.

One of the best things you can do for wildlife in your garden is to make sure there's water: a large pond is great, but a simple bird bath or trough is fine too. Water offers birds a space to drink and bathe, and attracts insects for them to feast on. Be sure to change the water every 1–2 days to prevent mosquitoes and to keep the water clean for bathing.

Other simple steps
Even how you garden makes a difference, so try to leave some "untidy" spaces that provide insect habitats, such as stacks of plant pots or logs, and patches of moss that are useful for nesting materials. Avoid pruning during the nesting season or when plants have berries, and never use pesticides or insecticides. Keep cats indoors and add decals or other markers to windows to protect birds.

Seed heads make a feast for blue jays

Don't be too tidy
Leave fallen apples, seed heads, and berries for the birds to feed on in winter.

The size of the entry hole in a nest box will determine which species makes it a home

Feeders and boxes

Bird feeders and nest boxes can turbo-charge the potential of your outdoor space as a supportive environment for birds, but choose them carefully and hang them wisely.

Choosing bird feeders

You have three key factors to consider: which type of feeder to get; what food to put in it; and where to hang it. Each choice you make will influence the species that visit and how attractive the feeder is to birds. Many types are designed to favor small birds, with springs to deter heavier ones, or are engineered to be squirrel proof—at least most of the time. Look at online reviews or ask other bird lovers for recommendations.

Choose from a variety of foods: nuts, seeds, grains, and suet balls or pellets will all meet the needs of different birds. Mix and match, or make your own, or provide many kinds of foods in separate feeders.

To avoid spreading bird flu and other diseases, it's vital to clean feeders regularly. Soak them in 10 percent bleach, rinse, and then dry thoroughly before refilling. If you see a dead bird, wash your feeders and wait a few weeks before rehanging them.

Where you hang your feeders can make a big difference; birds will not use a feeder if they don't think it's safe. Are there perches where they can stop and check for predators, or are there pets or people nearby that might scare them off? Create a feeding station with different food options if you have room, ideally somewhere where you can discreetly watch the birds feasting.

What's on the menu?
Different feeders are suited to particular foods. Make your own from recycled bottles, or try the latest squirrel-proof technology.

Offer suet to birds in the cold season in suet cages, but avoid suet in the summer when heat will melt it and soil bird feathers

Hanging nest boxes

Bird habitat has declined hugely, but putting up nest boxes offers birds a ready-made home. As with feeders, different types of nest boxes will attract different species, and where you site them is key. Whether you buy boxes or make your own, check the dimensions to make sure the holes are the right size for a particular species, and not too close to the ground. This reduces the risk of chicks fledging too soon. Research nest box positions for the birds you want to attract, whether up a tree, high on a wall, or on a fence—and empty the boxes of old nests each spring. Avoid using chemicals for cleaning or painting the interior of boxes.

Hanging a bird feeder is like giving birds a permanently fruiting tree to feed from

Hedge fund
Hedges offer shelter and nest sites for birds such as this wren. It keeps the nest clean and safe from predators by removing a fecal sac from its chick.

Choosing your plants

The plants you grow can actively support bird life, whether supplying food in the form of nectar or seeds, materials from which to build nests, shelter, or nest sites.

Flora for fauna

You can tailor what you plant to support a wide range of different birds, create specific conditions that are appealing to particular species, and grow plants that are native to your local area to support local birds. Nectar-rich flowers will attract pollinators such as beetles, flies, moths, and butterflies, many of which (including their larvae or caterpillars) are food for insect-eating birds. Don't forget that a particular flower may feed the adult insect, but their larvae or caterpillars might need other plants altogether.

Look beyond your garden to see what wildflowers and seed heads are buzzing with feeding activity, and maybe leave a little "wild patch" in your garden if you have space, or grow flowers that attract hummingbirds in a window box. Artificial grass is an ecological disaster, and even a flawless lawn is of little use to wildlife, so let the weeds, worms, and insects live in your lawn to give the flickers, catbirds, and robins a reason to visit you.

If you have room, try to create layers, by providing ground cover, shrubs, and a tree canopy. Favor hedges full of native berry-producing shrubs over fences, or at least plant climbers up your fences, such as trumpet honeysuckle, which offers nectar and berries, and Virginia creeper, which provides food when many other plants have finished flowering. Try to grow a range of plants that will provide food throughout the year.

Lawn larder
American robins and other birds gather earthworms and insects from wildlife-filled lawns to feed to their chicks.

Nest-building materials
Kind gardeners leave moss, twigs, and dry grass that can all be put to good use by titmice and other nesting parents.

Seeds to feed on
Leave the seed heads on plants after flowering, to provide a source of food for birds such as this American goldfinch.

Providing water

A small pond with some natural, native plantings offers birds and other creatures a home, but even a small, shallow bird bath on a terrace gives birds a place to drink and bathe.

Birds need water

Hydration is very important for birds, so any water feature you can offer will provide them with drinking water. They must also bathe regularly to keep their plumage in good condition. Some birds, such as barn and cliff swallows, need a nearby source of water to supply the wet mud from which they build their nests.

A shallow pond with natural, native plants provides a home for many creatures; it is a magnet for insects and, therefore, everything that feeds on insects, too, such as birds, frogs, and dragonflies. If you don't have much room, even a shallow barrel pond, trough, or small bird bath with gently sloping edges can offer birds a place to drink and bathe.

Use rainwater from rain barrels, if you can, rather than tap water (which may contain chlorine), and keep water levels topped off; it's unfair to get birds used to a food or drinking water supply and then forget it at a critical time. If you live in an area where the water might freeze in winter, you could put a floating ball on the water to prevent it from icing over completely, but never add chemicals such as antifreeze. "Fake" ponds using mirrors, or any large hanging outdoor mirror, too, can be lethal for birds; they may see a reflection in it (or in a window) and try to fly through it, often with fatal results.

Simple saucer
A plant saucer, topped off regularly, makes an ideal bird bath, but only put it at ground level if there are no predators or outdoor cats or dogs nearby.

A shallow bath
Birds use puddles when available, so your birdbath needs to be only as shallow as a puddle. Change the water frequently to prevent mosquitoes from breeding in it.

Pond life
Shallow ponds with mud patches and overhanging twigs and plants provide the ideal conditions for a thriving, bird-friendly ecosystem.

Habitats

With about 10,000 species in the world, birds will often surprise you by turning up in very unusual places, but thankfully they often stick to particular habitats that you can explore.

Keep your eyes peeled
Some birds are habitat specialists, but others are opportunists that fly over almost anywhere, so you never know what you might see.

Exploring bird habitats

This chapter outlines some of the primary habitat types and provides a simple field guide to the birds you might find there, from parks and gardens to sweeping shores and wild mountains.

Right place, right bird

Habitat requirements can be very broad or very precise. Birds that like large grasslands, such as meadowlarks, might find their requirements met in such varied habitats as fields, airports, and reclaimed strip mines. Likewise, killdeer might be found anywhere from school playgrounds, grassy parking lots, and sandy beaches to gravel rooftops. As long as there is food and shelter, many birds are likely to be found in multiple habitats.

Yet the basic need for the right habitat, at least when breeding, is a good clue to the likelihood of seeing any particular species, should you be in a wetland, a woodland, on hills or valleys, in farmland, or by the sea. There is a strong connection between a bird and its specific habitat. For some, habitat has a very narrow definition: to find breeding American bitterns, for example, you must look in a freshwater marsh—nowhere else will do.

Habitat as identification aid

It will become second nature to think of this connection between habitat and breeding birds when you see a bird you can't immediately recognize. Such a close relationship can quickly narrow down the options as to what birds you might be seeing in a particular habitat, and the field guides in this chapter will help you, although do note that the birds are not to scale. However much you try and categorize a bird, though, remember that they can fly wherever they want, so habitat alone won't provide all the clues; you also need to evaluate the visual and auditory details of a bird and take into account the season (see pp. 44–45).

Remember, when exploring habitats in different seasons, make sure you dress for the terrain and the elements. Be aware of the weather forecast, tide times, and other factors appropriate for the area you're exploring. Know the rules for visiting the countryside, sticking to public-access areas and being respectful of the rights of others. And, of course, keep the birdwatcher's code in mind: always put the interests of the birds first (see pp. 42–43).

Resident birds
Songbirds such as this American robin are completely at home in many gardens, which resemble their natural forest-edge habitat.

Gardens and balconies

Gardens, terraces, and balconies offer a variety of micro-habitats
for birds and also give you a convenient place in which you can
start practicing your birdwatching skills.

A little of everything

Once you start to watch out for them, you might be surprised by just how many birds
are sharing your outdoor space with you. From lawns full of worms and ants for doves,
thrushes, and blackbirds, to flower beds, shrubs, hedges, and trees for robins, titmice,
finches, sparrows, and hummingbirds, there is the potential in a garden for a great range
of birdlife. Even a small balcony can support plants that produce seeds or berries, or
attract insect life on which birds can feed. Hedges, shrubs, vine-covered walls, and
nest boxes also offer some birds a nest site, as do garden sheds, building eaves, and
old outbuildings; in summer, barn swallows and phoebes may nest there, so keep an
eye on the skies and atop nearby perches to learn your bird neighbors.

Some garden birds are common visitors, while others are seasonal migrants. At
sunrise in spring, the persistent singing of male songbirds to maintain their territory
is known as the dawn chorus. Once families have fledged, many must move away to
feed elsewhere if a garden can't support the additional numbers; birds may move away
until the population adjusts, returning to the garden once there are more berries, fallen
apples, or other food for them. Then, in winter, the avian residents are joined by a few
winter visitors, while the summer visitors migrate elsewhere until the next spring.

Nests and fledglings
In spring, watch for signs of
nests, such as adult American
robins flying in and out of a
hedge to feed their brood.

Fall resources
Gardens can offer food when
natural habitats are depleted.
Visitors such as this cedar
waxwing might search of berries.

Winter refuge
If snow makes feeding difficult
in open fields and wild shrub
berries have all gone, you may
attract visitors such as bluebirds.

Birds of garden spaces

The birds visiting your outdoor space will vary depending on where you live, on the time of year, and on the trees, bushes, and plants growing there.

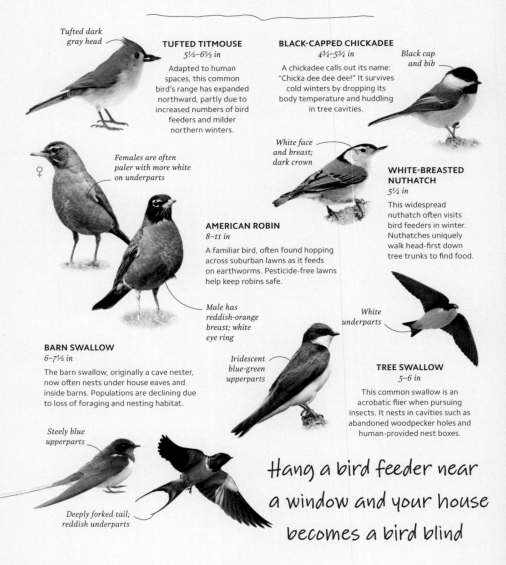

Tufted dark gray head

TUFTED TITMOUSE
5½–6⅓ in

Adapted to human spaces, this common bird's range has expanded northward, partly due to increased numbers of bird feeders and milder northern winters.

BLACK-CAPPED CHICKADEE
4¾–5¾ in

A chickadee calls out its name: "Chicka dee dee dee!" It survives cold winters by dropping its body temperature and huddling in tree cavities.

Black cap and bib

Females are often paler with more white on underparts

White face and breast; dark crown

WHITE-BREASTED NUTHATCH
5¼ in

This widespread nuthatch often visits bird feeders in winter. Nuthatches uniquely walk head-first down tree trunks to find food.

AMERICAN ROBIN
8–11 in

A familiar bird, often found hopping across suburban lawns as it feeds on earthworms. Pesticide-free lawns help keep robins safe.

Male has reddish-orange breast; white eye ring

White underparts

BARN SWALLOW
6–7½ in

The barn swallow, originally a cave nester, now often nests under house eaves and inside barns. Populations are declining due to loss of foraging and nesting habitat.

Iridescent blue-green upperparts

TREE SWALLOW
5–6 in

This common swallow is an acrobatic flier when pursuing insects. It nests in cavities such as abandoned woodpecker holes and human-provided nest boxes.

Steely blue upperparts

Deeply forked tail; reddish underparts

Hang a bird feeder near a window and your house becomes a bird blind

GRAY CATBIRD
8–9½ in

In addition to its mewing calls, a gray catbird can mimic dozens of other species. It nests in shrubs in suburban and urban areas.

Gray overall with a long tail

DOWNY WOODPECKER
6–7 in

The smallest US woodpecker forages for insects on tree trunks. It drums on trees to attract a mate and claim a territory.

Male has a black bib and gray crown

Females are duller yellow or olive

Breeding males have sunny yellow plumage

HOUSE SPARROW
6¼ in

A noisy, sociable little bird that likes dense thickets and roof tiles and gutters, it is often found around people.

AMERICAN GOLDFINCH
4¼–5 in

Among summer's last birds to nest and breed, this finch forages in twittering flocks, feeding almost entirely on small seeds.

HOUSE FINCH
5–6 in

This social, common feeder bird has a relatively large, conical bill for eating seeds, which it shells in rapid, crushing bites.

Female is unmarked below, with a pale stripe behind the eye

Glossy, with a green and purple sheen

STARLING
7¾–9 in

The seemingly black feathers of this bird have an iridescent sheen. See it bathing, feeding on the lawn, or flocking in noisy, chattering groups.

BLUE JAY
9½–12 in

Acorns are a favorite food for this common feeder bird, known for its loud "jay!" call. Slightly larger Steller's Jays are found in the west.

Blue wings, tail, and crest; white wing bars

HOUSE WREN
4½ in

Feeding almost entirely on insects, this tiny bird can be recognized by its loud, bubbly song and often-cocked tail.

NORTHERN FLICKER
11–12¼ in

This ground foraging bird has two forms: yellow-shafted and red-shafted, which are distinguishable in flight by their underwing colors.

Brown back with black barring

Brown body with narrow black bars on wings and tail

Gray with a long tail

MOURNING DOVE
9–13½ in

Named for its mournful call, this ground feeding bird is one of the most abundant US birds. It stores seeds in its crop to eat anytime.

Canada geese
These large North American geese are relatively bold, curious, and aggressive around their human neighbors.

Parks and park lakes

You can learn a lot about birds in your local parks, where they'll be relatively relaxed around people. This gives you a chance to hone your bird identification skills and study them closely.

Up close and personal

With people always around, park birds are mostly tame, opportunistic, and adaptable. Other than in a backyard, this is commonly the easiest habitat in which to practice birdwatching and see different species.

Visit regularly through the seasons and you can study the various plumages of a species. You can compare those of a mallard, for example—juvenile, female, and the male in winter and in summer, when it looks more like a female but keeps the yellow beak and black-and-white tail. Look at the gulls, also showing a variety of plumages according to age and season, but with no difference between the sexes. Then there are coots and gallinules; although they keep the same plumage all year, the juvenile plumage is different from the adult's, so you can learn to identify the young ones.

Towhees and sparrows come for crumbs, while flycatchers and vireos keep their distance but are still there to be seen and heard. You'll soon learn the songs of cardinals and titmice and how to tell a downy woodpecker from a hairy woodpecker. There is plenty to enjoy but also plenty of opportunity to practice your identification skills if you take the time to look and listen.

Spring chicks
In spring, look for mallards shepherding their orderly brood of ducklings out onto the water.

Flashy cardinal
The cardinal prefers to hide in shrubs and trees but will venture out for sunflower seeds.

Nesting in style
Water bird nests might be on solid ground or afloat on the water. Canada geese nest on dry land.

Birds of parks and park lakes

Visit your local park to practice identifying birds; a park lake, for example, can help you learn to distinguish common water birds that may be more abundant elsewhere, but also farther from you.

MUTE SWAN
50–59¾ in

Happy by or on the water, this huge, orange-beaked swan will come near for crumbs – but gives a warning hiss if you get too close.

Black knob on bill

Adult bill is orange; juvenile bill is gray

White forehead and bill

AMERICAN COOT
15½–17 in

A medium-sized black bird with a white face and beak, usually found walking by, or swimming and diving in, open water.

Bright reddish cap, white eyebrow

CHIPPING SPARROW
5¼ in

A sharp "chip!" call gives this small sparrow its name. It is often found near trees that surround open, grassy parks and backyards.

NORTHERN MOCKINGBIRD
8½–10 in

This bird's song can imitate 100 other bird species. Its white "wing flash" display is used in courtship and may startle insects into revealing themselves.

Gray with white wing patches

Males bright yellow overall

YELLOW WARBLER
5 in

By May, this warbler's "sweet sweet, sweet, I'm so sweet" song can be heard across North America as it arrives for summer.

Head to the park early in the morning, before it gets too busy, to see maximum bird activity

Pale gray back; black band on yellow bill

RING-BILLED GULL
17–21½ in

A common sight in parking lots and picnic areas, especially near lakes and reservoirs, this gull often scavenges from garbage.

Male bill is bright yellow; female bill is orange and brown

MALLARD
19⅔–25½ in

A coarse "quack" helps you identify this large, orange-legged duck. The male is brightly colored; the female is streaky brown with a blue wing patch.

Black head and neck, with white chinstrap

Gray-brown back; white rear

CANADA GOOSE
30–43⅓ in

Often found grazing on short grass by the waterside, the black-necked Canada goose is large, with a loud honk.

Males glossy blue-black overall

PURPLE MARTIN
7–8 in

The largest of all North American swallows, this martin is mostly found in the east, where they nest in birdhouses. In the west they nest in woodpecker holes.

Square red forehead shield

Glossy brown back

GREEN HERON
16–18 in

A solitary, bird of dense, thicketed wetlands, this heron is often seen flying away from a disturbance with a loud, squawking "keow!"

COMMON GALLINULE
12⅔–13¾ in

Equally at home on land and water, this bird's long toes allow it to walk easily over floating plants and soft mud.

Long gray shaggy-plumed neck; blue-gray body

GREAT BLUE HERON
38¼–54 in

Flying in slow motion, this heron keeps its long neck tucked and legs trailing. On land, it stands motionless in shallow water, patiently awaiting its prey.

SPOTTED SANDPIPER
7¼–8 in

With a quick walking pace, constant tail-bobbing, and habit of flying low over the water, this short-legged sandpiper is widespread on shores of lakes, ponds, and rivers.

White underparts with dark spots on breeding birds

Urban areas and landfills

Despite the constant hum of activity in cities and towns, some birds manage to make themselves at home on patches of green space, building roofs, and even parking lots or landfills.

Finding a way to thrive

Birds are more adaptable than you might think. Kestrels and the once-rare peregrine falcon, originally at home on cliff tops and rocky ridges, have learned to substitute tall building ledges high over the city for nesting and feed on urban insects and rodents. The plentiful pigeon population is "feral," domesticated from wild rock doves long ago, but since gone back to the wild; "pure" rock doves are now rare.

Gulls nest on flat roofs and eat scraps even in the busiest downtown streets. The garbage we throw away can contain a lot of food for birds. It attracts other creatures, too, which some birds can eat. Even tarmac, concrete, and asphalt can house insects on which birds can feed. Blackbirds pick dead flies from parked cars, and cardinals attack their reflections in car mirrors. You might even hear the song of a mockingbird if it settles on a factory or railroad station roof. Unused land that becomes overgrown with thistles, brambles, and other plants can host a greater variety of birdlife, especially in fall and winter, when busy flocks of goldfinches, house finches, and house sparrows appear.

City hunters
Red-tailed hawks originally nested in trees but have adapted to nest on the high ledges of city buildings.

Street scavengers
Gulls and pigeons are very opportunistic and adaptable, finding plenty to eat among the foods we humans discard.

Parking lot nesters
Killdeer have adapted to nest in urban habitats such as playgrounds, gravel parking lots, and even flat gravel rooftops.

Nest materials
Although American robins were originally forest birds, they now build their nests wherever people—and their debris—are found.

ROCK PIGEON
11¾–14¼ in

This fast, bold bird has varied colors and patterns. Descended from the wild rock dove, it is extremely well adapted to urban living.

HOUSE SPARROW
6¼ in

Introduced to New York in 1850, these hardy birds are now ubiquitous throughout North America, especially in urban areas.

Breeding males have black wings and cap

May be gray, white, brown, or patchwork colors

AMERICAN GOLDFINCH
4¼–5 in

This finch is often seen near feeders and around overgrown areas where there are plenty seeds and nesting sites.

Males have a bright orange-red forehead, rump, and breast

HOUSE FINCH
5–6 in

This colorful songbird nests close to human homes, tucking its grass nest into house crevices.

CHIMNEY SWIFT
4⅗–6 in

Described as "flying cigars," this swift feeds, drinks, and bathes on the wing. It depends upon human-made structures for nesting.

Dark brown overall with long wings and short square tail

Deeply forked tail

Short, notched tail

Steely blue upperparts and deeply forked tail

BARN SWALLOW
6–7½ in

After returning from winter in South America, this graceful bird uses mud to build a nest under house eaves.

TREE SWALLOW
5–6 in

Often seen around nest boxes, this common swallow will search compost for egg shells during breeding season when it needs extra calcium.

Birds of urban areas and landfills

On "waste" or abandoned ground and rooftops, you'll find birds living and foraging. Gulls—although they are seabirds—are some of the most successful at adapting. They feed on landfills and even nest on roofs, far from their coastal strongholds.

Look carefully and you may see a
kestrel or swift soaring overhead,
or a mourning dove on the path

Mostly black, with a white belly and white patches

White head and body; gray upperparts

The glossy black feathers shimmer with greens and blues

RING-BILLED GULL
17–21½ in

Often seen around landfills, this gull has become used to feeding on almost any food it can find.

BLACK-BILLED MAGPIE
17⅔–23⅔ in

This member of the crow family, with its unmistakable black-and-white plumage, can often be found in urban habitats, searching for food.

Red spot near tip of bill is common

Pale gray back and wings

Wing tips are black with white spots

Small unfeathered red head

Dark brown back, black underparts

HERRING GULL
21½–25½ in

A large gull with pink legs, the herring gull is bold and loud. A native of cliffs, it has adapted to urban ledges and roofs.

TURKEY VULTURE
25–32 in

Flying turkey vultures hold their wings in a V shape. This bird uses its fine-tuned sense of smell to find dead animals, often feasting on roadkill.

Long thick bill

COMMON RAVEN
22–27¼ in

Among the most intelligent birds, the raven can learn, adapt, and solve problems quickly. It often scavenges on landfills.

Black overall

AMERICAN CROW
15¾–21 in

Common in most habitats, the crow's loud "caw!" is one of the most familiar bird calls. It is among the smartest and most social birds.

Rocky shores, cliffs, and open sea

A big seabird colony is alive with noise and movement—it even smells different. Add the open sea and the sky, and you have one of the most exciting places to birdwatch.

Seabird cities

Craggy shorelines are harsh places yet invaluable for nesting seabirds. Flat rocks, ledges, and deep cavities attract different species, all of which feed out at sea but must find a safe place to lay their eggs.

On cliffs and islands, you may see cormorants and gulls—including kittiwakes. Perhaps you will find fulmars and an assortment of auks: murres (on ledges); razorbills (often in natural cavities); and puffins (nesting in deeper burrows). These auks lay eggs directly onto bare rock, while kittiwakes build bulky nests of mud and grass to hold their eggs. Cliffs become white with droppings by midsummer.

In cavities and old rabbit holes, there may be petrels and shearwaters, which cannot walk well and come to the nest only after dark. You might need to book an organized expedition to see those, but they are often visible offshore in the daytime.

Between the rocks, there may be patches of shoreline, which can be covered in seaweed. This offers places for some shorebirds to feed, but the numbers and variety are never as high as you'll see on muddy coasts.

On the rock face
Coastal cliffs are a key stronghold for the agile, powerful peregrine falcon, which breeds high on the rocky ledges.

Expert divers
Gathering in huge, noisy colonies on coastal rocks, gannets feed on fish, diving headfirst into the sea to catch their food.

Hardy shorebirds
Purple sandpipers can be seen picking over seaweed-covered rocks in search of crustaceans and mollusks to eat.

Bird stacks
In the breeding season, rock "stacks" can be completely taken over by noisy colonies of nesting seabirds.

Black plumage becomes mottled in winter

BLACK GUILLEMOT
11¾–12⅔ in

Look for these on rocky islets, not sheer cliffs. Pairs bob around inshore or sit on rocks, revealing bright red legs.

Brown head turns white with dark stripe in winter

COMMON MURRE
15–17 in

Often seen upright, squatting on a ledge, this bird is buoyant on the water, with a whirring, heavy flight over the water.

Back is gray-brown with curled whitish fringes

PURPLE SANDPIPER
8¼ in

A small, dark bird with dull yellow legs, this wader visits in winter to feed on weedy, wave-splashed rocks and drifts of seaweed.

RAZORBILL
17 in

This bird typically shares breeding colonies with murres but prefers the shady cavities. In winter, its black head turns white with a black cap.

Thick black bill with white lines

Glossy black overall

COMMON RAVEN
22–27¼ in

This predatory bird has been known to steal an egg or young chick from the nests of other seabirds.

Two black bars on a pale wing

ROCK PIGEON
11¾–14½ in

This widespread feral bird has a broad body and small head. In coastal areas, it nests on the ledges of tall, rocky cliffs.

Pale stripe over eye and under cheek

SONG SPARROW
4⅔–6⅔ in

Courting males sing a melodious song on an exposed perch at eye level. In winter, song sparrows can eat several thousand tiny weed seeds per hour.

BLACK-LEGGED KITTIWAKE
15–16 in

This gull spends all winter at sea, then nests on sheer cliffs and ledges. Its loud "kit-ti-wake" call rings from the rocks.

White below, with silvery-gray upper parts

Black triangle on wingtip

NORTHERN FULMAR
15⅓–19⅔ in

Although it resembles a medium-sized gull, the stiff-winged, gray-tailed fulmar is unrelated. It nests on rocky cliffs but is otherwise to be found at sea.

Thick bill has tubular nostrils

Sharp-edged translucent wings

ARCTIC TERN
11¾–15⅓ in

An elegant bird with a long tail, very short red legs, and a blood-red beak, this tern nests on shingle or rocks. It will dive-bomb intruders, so keep your distance!

Birds of rocky shores, cliffs, and open sea

Look offshore for birds flying low over the sea, moving to and from their feeding areas, or in the nooks and crannies along the shoreline. In spring, train your binoculars on the rocky cliffs to spot their nesting sites.

DOUBLE-CRESTED CORMORANT
28–35 in

A courting male will choose a nest site and stand there, bill pointed to the sky, showing off its crests and brightly colored face and eyes.

Orange face, bright teal-blue eyes

Black overall

Long, sloping forehead

COMMON EIDER
19½–28 in

The largest sea duck in North America, eiders raft in large floating flocks as they dive for mollusks. Famously warm, eiderdown keeps their chicks warm.

Distinctive yellow head

NORTHERN GANNET
36¾–43⅓ in

A seabird with a gleaming white body and long, black-tipped wings, it can be found in huge, noisy, crowded colonies on cliffs.

Dark head and black moustache, with white cheeks

PEREGRINE FALCON
14½–19⅓ in

This bird of prey nests on cliffs and roams widely in search of food, soaring with short bursts of quick, stiff wingbeats.

Gray face edged with black cap and neck

Colorful bill to attract a mate

ATLANTIC PUFFIN
10¼–11⅓ in

Waddling on orange legs, the puffin nests in burrows rather than on open cliff ledges and spends winter at sea.

Take care of your binoculars—keep them dry and protected from salty sea spray

Feats of flying
Dunlins roost together on the shoreline in the thousands at high tide. If you're lucky, you might see aerobatic displays as flocks arrive to roost.

Sandy shores

Many birds live in shallow offshore bays and along sandy shorelines, often fringed by grass-covered dunes, but beaches can be too busy with human activity, so many nesting birds are found in protected natural areas.

Open spaces and big skies

Although wide, sandy beaches have fewer birds of fewer kinds compared with muddy estuaries, you'll still find plenty of action on land and in the air. On the shores, there may be plovers, laughing gulls, common terns, and willets.

From fall to spring, you'll see visiting shorebirds, particularly sanderlings, dunlins, turnstones, and oystercatchers. They and many other birds may choose a coastal lagoon as their high-tide roost, and flocks should not be disturbed while they're resting, but you can sometimes get a good view from the dunes with a scope or binoculars.

Down at the water's edge, sanderlings dart in and out with the waves, while turnstones flip over seaweed and pebbles along the wrack line to hunt for food beneath. These water birds, too, are sensitive to disturbance and need to be left in peace if they are to nest successfully. Sanderlings are absent only in midsummer, which is also when some species of terns feed and nest inland on freshwater lakes.

Look offshore to see diving ducks, such as eiders, black scoters, and in winter, long-tailed ducks feeding on shellfish. Often, they appear only as the swell rises, or when they fly low over the waves in straggling lines.

On the waterline
When not roosting in tight flocks, pearl-and-silver winter sanderlings can be seen feeding rapidly, running along the water's edge.

Handsome gulls
Although laughing gulls nest on islands and marshes, you can also see them feeding on sandy beaches.

Offshore swimmers
Look for black scoters swimming just offshore. Male scoters are black, but females are browner and have a pale face.

Long, thick bill

WILLET
12½–16½ in

The willet picks, probes, and swishes underwater with its straight bill, searching for crustaceans and other prey.

MARBLED GODWIT
16½–19 in

Open habitats, such as mudflats and floodplains, make this shorebird a familiar sight as it feeds and roosts on its coastal wintering grounds.

Very long, slightly upturned bill

Dark patch on shoulder

SANDERLING
7–7¾ in

Watch this little wader as it runs along the tide line, dodging waves and looking for food.

Black legs

Pale gray wings

Checkered upper parts; breeding male has a black belly

Black cap

BLACK-BELLIED PLOVER
11–11⅓ in

This plover migrates from nesting sites in tundra to coastal beaches in the Caribbean Islands and northern South America.

Red bill with dark tip

CASPIAN TERN
18½–21½ in

The world's largest tern, the Caspian tern aggressively defends its nesting territory. Its call is a hoarse, deep "kraaa kraaa."

White body

COMMON TERN
12¼–15 in

This widespread, medium-sized tern has a pointed orange bill with a black tip. It does not walk easily on its short red legs but hovers over the water before diving for fish.

Long tail streamers resemble a swallow's in flight

Yellow bill and a black cap

LEAST TERN
8½–9 in

The smallest tern, this bird darts over the water, near the shoreline, as it searches for small fish to feed on.

Check when high tide is, to make sure you don't get stranded

GREAT BLACK-BACKED GULL
28–31 in

The largest gull, with a massive head and bill, this bird is majestic and powerful in flight, with long glides on bowed wings.

Legs are dull pale pink

LONG-BILLED CURLEW
19⅔–25⅔ in

The largest North American shorebird. It is often seen away from the shore, on dry grasslands in summer and on prairies in winter.

Males black with yellow-orange knob on black bill

BLACK SCOTER
17–19⅓ in

Found in dense flocks offshore or flying in long undulating lines low over the sea, this large, dark duck is bulky but elegant.

Male has a long black tail, absent in females

LONG-TAILED DUCK
15¾–18½ in

The plumage of this winter visitor changes over the season. It flies low over the sea, flocks on the water, and dives for food.

RED-BREASTED MERGANSER
20–25 in

A frequent diver and efficient hunter of fish, this large, elongated, angular duck gathers in groups or larger flocks offshore.

Long, serrated bill is good for gripping fish

White eye ring

BLACK SKIMMER
15½–19½ in

This seabird's knifelike bill features a lower mandible about an inch longer than the upper—perfect for skimming the sea surface and snapping shut on prey.

Short orange legs

RUDDY TURNSTONE
6⅓–8⅓ in

This bird is seen on beaches, turning over pebbles and seaweed to unearth crustaceans and other prey beneath.

Brownish above; white below

SEMIPALMATED PLOVER
6¾–7½ in

On a quiet sandy beach between fall and spring, there might be dozens of these small birds, asleep in sandy depressions. Flocks may number up to 1,000 birds.

GREATER YELLOWLEGS
11½–13 in

Often seen running frantically in various directions in pursuit of small prey, this shorebird is among the first northbound migrants to arrive in spring.

Birds of sandy shores

Sandy beaches, bays, and coastal lagoons are popular with human visitors, but some birds manage to thrive too. Visit at low tide, when the birds are feeding on the exposed wrack line, or as the incoming tide pushes flocks up to the high-water mark.

Estuaries

Estuaries combine several habitats, each offering opportunities for watching different birds through the year. Be careful not to disturb resting flocks at high tide and also to keep safe in areas with fast-rising water and deep muddy creeks.

Wide, open spaces

Large estuaries may have thousands of birds, but they can be spread out across this big, broad habitat, so timing can make a huge difference in how many of them you actually see. Try to time your visits for an incoming tide, when you'll see the birds move from feeding areas to roosts. You will see dense flocks of many species, but as the tide falls again they disperse and become harder to identify from a distance. At low tide you'll see shorebirds combing the mudflats in search of crustaceans, mollusks, and worms.

Listen to the calls. Shorebirds nearly always call in flight, making identification so much easier. In winter, the chatter of huge flocks of geese fills the air, and other birds may join in the daily movements, coming to the salt marsh to roost and moving off to feed, sometimes inland (as with geese) or out at the water's edge. At dusk, flocks of Canada geese create wonderful spectacles against evening skies.

In summer, estuarine marshes may have breeding laughing gulls, willets, and swamp sparrows. And, if they are not disturbed by humans and predators, you may see piping plovers, gulls, and terns nesting on sandbars and ridges.

Ready to breed
In spring, before heading north to breed, knots develop a rich "red" breeding plumage.

Unique beak
In the shallows, American avocets sweep their upturned bill through the water to detect food.

Winter geese
Although several species of geese use the marsh, the brant feed out on the mudflats at low tides.

Coming in for landing
Canada geese find safety from predators at night by roosting together on open water, even when it is covered in ice.

Birds of estuaries

On the water, you may see gulls, diving ducks, and grebes, while marshes and muddy creeks will have more dabbling ducks and geese. At low tide, look for shorebirds on the mudflats too.

AMERICAN WIGEON
17½–23 in

An opportunist that feeds on vegetation dislodged by other ducks, this mid-sized dabbling duck is common and widespread.

Male has brown head with white neck-stripe

NORTHERN PINTAIL
20–30 in

Out on the saltmarsh, you may see the elegant, long-necked pintail, a quiet dabbling duck. Look for the white breast and long tail of the males.

Brown breast and flanks; breeding male has cream-colored forehead

TUNDRA SWAN
47¼–58 in

Nesting in the Arctic tundra, this bird is North America's most widespread, and also smallest, swan. Its call is a high-pitched, yodeling "hoo hooo."

Yellow facial patch next to eye

GREATER WHITE-FRONTED GOOSE
25¼–30¾ in

White markings on the forehead and around the bill give this winter visitor its name. Flocks fly in long lines and V-shapes, with a loud, yodeling chorus.

Black bars across the belly

Orange legs

BRANT
22–26 in

Small-billed, dark, and stocky, this sea goose has a black neck and head. It flies over estuaries with a distinctive low, guttural call.

Brown wings and back

CANADA GOOSE
30–43⅓ in

The Canada goose is the most familiar, common, and widespread goose in North America. It can be found swimming in open water during summer months.

Chunky grayish-brown body

Pale-bellied on the east coast; black-bellied on the west coast

RUDDY TURNSTONE
6⅓–8⅓ in

This stocky bird migrates from the arctic tundra to North American coasts. It wades only into shallow water.

HUDSONIAN GODWIT
14–16 in

This bird undertakes a remarkable migration from the Alaskan and Canadian tundra to southern South America—nearly 10,000 miles.

Chestnut underneath

DUNLIN
6⅓–8⅔ in

Probing for food with its slender bill, the dunlin has a gray winter plumage that becomes brighter in spring.

WILLET
12⅓–16⅓ in

This easy-to-spot bird feeds on the shoreline and mudflats, during the day and night, on insects, worms, snails, and crustaceans.

Slender bill

LESSER YELLOWLEGS
11⅓–13 in

Shorter than the great yellowlegs, this medium-sized shorebird forages at night with its neck outstretched.

Cinnamon head and neck on breeding birds

AMERICAN AVOCET
17–18⅓ in

The plumage pattern of this graceful shorebird is striking in flight. Its long, thin, upturned bill makes it recognizable when foraging.

WHIMBREL
17–18 in

Slightly smaller than a curlew, the whimbrel has a striped head and quick, trilling call note. In spring, flocks pass offshore or rest on salt marsh.

BLACK-BELLIED PLOVER
11–11⅓ in

Named for the breeding male's black belly, this plover's bulky appearance, and upright stance, make it fairly conspicuous.

Red breast and face in breeding season

RED KNOT
9–10 in

In winter, this plump bird forages on the edges of estuaries and mudflats for clams, mussels, and their larvae. It makes quick picking movements similar to sandpipers.

AMERICAN OYSTERCATCHER
15⅓–17⅓ in

Easy to identify with its carrotlike bill and bold white wing bars, this large shorebird has a loud, descending "wheeu" call.

Long red-orange bill

White throat band
Pinkish legs

Stay on the paths to avoid marshy ground and, in spring, to make sure you don't disturb any nesting birds

Rivers

From silvery trickles of cold water in the uplands to rushing torrents over rocky riverbeds to slow, meandering waterways nearing the sea, rivers offer a variety of habitats to suit many different types of birds.

Different speeds for different species

As rivers make their way from their source, they commonly flow over different soils and rocks, gathering speed and then perhaps slowing as they broaden out. They support a variety of vegetation, invertebrates, and fish along the way—and beside their banks will be birds hunting among those food sources. Few birds can adapt to them all, so visit a range of rivers to fully explore the species that make rivers their home.

Upland streams can be good in summer, with beautifully crystal-clear waters that have been filtered through rock and soil. Common mergansers nest in tree cavities along rivers and spotted sandpipers flit along the shore, bobbing their tails in a conspicuous way. Mountain streams in western states are home to American dippers. This unique songbird feeds underwater, even walking on the river bottom.

Kingfishers are often overlooked as they are remarkably inconspicuous in the dappled waterside light until they let out with their long, rattlelike call. Only broad, still stretches of river are used by fish-eating common mergansers and wood ducks, but you can find green herons perched on overhanging branches near the water. Look to the slow-moving edges of larger rivers to see great blue herons patiently waiting for fish to swim within range.

Riverbank nests
In spring, young merganser chicks hitch a ride on their mother's back. Look out for their nests in riverside trees.

Spotting spots
By the river, watch for jaunty spotted sandpipers; they have a bouncy walk and their polka-dot breast gives them their name.

Snowy stalkers
In western and southern rivers, coastal marshes, and beaches, watch for snowy egrets hunting for crustaceans and small fish.

A sudden strike
On a branch overhanging a river, you may spot a belted kingfisher patiently watching and waiting. If you're lucky, you might see it suddenly dive for a minnow.

BELTED KINGFISHER
11–14 in

A loud, long rattle in flight often makes this aquatic bird easier to hear than see. A large bill helps catch and hold slippery fish.

Females have a chestnut breastband

Slate blue upper body and white collar

Spots disappear after the breeding season

SPOTTED SANDPIPER
7¼–8 in

Characterized by its constant teetering and tail bobbing, this small sandpiper is North America's most widespread shorebird.

BALTIMORE ORIOLE
6⅔–7½ in

Beloved for its brilliant colors, melodious song, and tolerance of humans, this songbird may be heard around river banks singing high in the trees.

Black back and bright orange underparts

BANK SWALLOW
4¾–5⅓ in

The smallest North American swallow, it sometimes forms noisy nesting colonies of hundreds, which can be found in the banks of rivers and streams.

WARBLING VIREO
5⅓ in

Named for its cheerful warbling song and warbler-like appearance, this vireo is likely to be seen perched in trees lining streams.

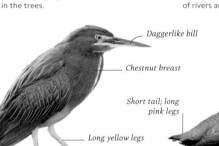

Daggerlike bill

Chestnut breast

Short tail; long pink legs

Long yellow legs

Slate gray all over

Droopy crest feathers and black eyestripe

GREEN HERON
16–18 in

This heron waits in the shallows of rivers, sometimes hidden by vegetation, to surprise fish as they swim by. It has also been known to lure fish with twigs or insects.

AMERICAN DIPPER
5½–8 in

An aquatic songbird, dippers are named for their habit of bobbing up and down while feeding on the bottom of fast-moving, rocky streams.

Yellow bill

GREAT BLUE HERON
38¼–54 in

The bright white neck of this very large bird is typically sunk into its shoulders; in flight, its broad, arched wings flap languidly and its long legs stretch out behind.

Black cap, white forehead, yellow bill

LEAST TERN
8½–9 in

During breeding season, this little tern dives into the open waters of broad rivers in search of small fish to feed on, or bring back to the nest.

Stands immobile in the shallows, waiting for prey

Birds of rivers

Over fast-flowing waters, you may see little insect-feeding birds darting around, while the wading, diving, and dabbling waterfowl are at home on slower waters. Increasingly, the cormorant is making its home inland too.

White eye ring

SOLITARY SANDPIPER
7¼–9 in

Moving cautiously along wetland margins, this sandpiper constantly bobs its head when feeding and flies directly upward when disturbed.

Breeding males have a multicolored body

WOOD DUCK
18½–21½ in

The breeding male's gaudy plumage is easy to recognize. The only waterfowl that raises two broods each season, wood ducks prefer wetlands surrounded by trees.

DOUBLE-CRESTED CORMORANT
28–35 in

When fishing, this cormorant dives from the surface to chase fish underwater. Afterward, it can be seen resting on rocks and spreading its wings out to dry.

Male has glossy green breeding plumage

MALLARD
19⅗–25½ in

This familiar orange-legged duck feeds while it is in the water by dipping its head below the surface.

Long neck and black overall

COMMON MERGANSER
21⅓–28 in ♀

Widespread, especially in the north, this large fish-eater is often seen on small rivers, using its serrated bill to catch fish underwater.

Females have a shaggy rusty head; males have an iridescent dark green head

From source to sea, one river alone can offer a huge range of habitats for birds

Freshwater marshes

In these permanently damp or flooded places, cattail, sedges, and wetland plants thrive, along with birds highly adapted to living on, around, and above the water margins.

Hide and seek

The edge of a marsh is a rewarding place for birds and birdwatcher alike. Dense wetland vegetation often thins out at the edge, with little openings, ditches, and streams among the grass and sedge. These allow in light for plants and insects, while also offering cover for fish-eating birds such as American bitterns and Virginia rails.

Look in nearby willows for migrants such as small warblers and flycatchers. They may be joined by familiar acrobatic species such as kinglets and gnatcatchers. On the waterline beneath, American coots and common gallinules will feed, alongside American black ducks and gadwalls, Virginia rails, and American bitterns, although you're more likely to hear than see these elusive marsh dwellers, as their plumage camouflages them perfectly and they hide deep among the reed stems. In fall, red-winged blackbirds often flock to marshes at night to roost in vast numbers where they are safe from predators.

Marsh camouflage
Bitterns hide in marshes
and build raised nests
where they incubate their
eggs. In spring, listen for
their booming calls.

Insect feeders
Often seen on cattails,
red-winged blackbirds feed
their young with the
insects that are abundant
in marsh habitats.

Hidden nests
Northern harriers nest on
the ground, but they find
safety in dense patches of
cattails where their nests
are well hidden.

Birds that rely on marshes are naturally rare and localized. Marsh wrens and swamp
sparrows, for example, feed and nest only within marshes, while black terns sometimes
nest on muskrat platforms or lodges. In northern marshes, least bitterns may breed,
and then migrate long distances to warmer marshes farther south before winter to
avoid ice. In spring, Northern harriers will nest in small patches of marsh and hunt for
mice and voles over adjacent open ground.

Gigantic flocks
Red-winged blackbird
flocks can number in the
thousands or millions
when they return to their
marsh roosts at dusk.

Brown, streaky plumage

Orange-yellow bill

GREAT EGRET
37–41 in

This tall bird hunts in marshes for small fish, amphibians, and invertebrates. It wades into the water and waits for prey to come near.

AMERICAN BITTERN
23⅔–33½ in

Camouflage plumage and secretive behavior help this bittern blend into thickly vegetated wetlands. It has a deep, resonant "pumper-unk" call.

Eye blends in with black skin and bill

TRUMPETER SWAN
54⅓–62¼ in

North America's heaviest waterfowl, its resonant "oh OH" call is reminiscent of a French horn.

White, snakelike neck

GREAT BLUE HERON
38¼–54 in

Standing like a statue in the shallows, with its neck stiffly extended or snakily hunched into its shoulders, this large heron waits patiently for a meal to swim by.

Long, dull legs

V-shaped wings

Buffy marbled upperparts

SHORT-EARED OWL
13½–16 in

On cloudy days or near dusk, this owl soars back and forth low over open fields. Unlike most owls, it builds its own nest—a scrape on the ground.

Males blue-gray; females dark brown

NORTHERN HARRIER
18–20 in

An owl-like face containing stiff feathers helps this hawk channel in sounds from prey while flying low over open wet fields.

Glossy brown back

White undertail

COMMON GALLINULE
12⅔–13¾ in

This medium-sized bird hides in the thick vegetation of marshes but is easily found by its whinnying and clucking noises.

Watch the "in between" spaces, where water and vegetation meet— that's where many birds like to hide

Birds of the marshes

Freshwater marshes come to life with warblers and wagtails in summer, but the winter birds can also be exciting. Look among the reeds and waterline vegetation for signs of activity.

Breeding male has bright red shoulder patches

Male has a yellow head

YELLOW-HEADED BLACKBIRD
8–11 in

Large, noisy nesting colonies of this blackbird can be found in western cattail marshes and prairie wetlands.

RED-WINGED BLACKBIRD
7–10 in

This abundant blackbird is conspicuous in marshy habitats. Males enthusiastically sing "oak-a-ree!" from atop cattails in spring.

COMMON YELLOWTHROAT
5 in

Its loud, distinctive "WITCH-a-tee, WITCH-a tee" song makes this common warbler easy to recognize.

Tan upperparts with dark streaks

MARSH WREN
4–5½ in

Singing both day and night, the male marsh wren performs aerial courtship and constructs "dummy" nests that may demonstrate his fitness to potential mates.

SWAMP SPARROW
5–6 in

Often seen darting into its dense marshes, this sparrow has a gray, faintly streaked breast and rusty-edged wing feathers.

Downward curved bill with orange base

PECTORAL SANDPIPER
7½–9 in

Migrating from its South American wintering grounds to high Arctic breeding grounds, the pectoral sandpiper travels about 19,000 miles each year.

Slightly downcurved red bill

VIRGINIA RAIL
8–10⅔ in

Using its "thin as a rail" body to push apart thick, reedy vegetation, this freshwater marsh dweller's grunting "oinks" are heard more often than the bird is seen.

Long, tapered bill

WILSON'S SNIPE
10–11 in

In nocturnal display flights, this well-camouflaged sandpiper flies up, then descends quickly, making eerie sounds through its tail feathers.

SORA
8–10 in

During breeding season, this rail may be seen along the edges of freshwater marshes. Listen for its horselike whinny.

Gray breast and brown upperparts

Lakes, reservoirs, and gravel pits

Natural lakes, flooded gravel pits, and reservoirs all offer wetland bird habitats that may have observation blinds built beside them, so you can watch the birds without disturbing them.

Sit and watch

Wetland areas lend themselves to permanent public observation blinds, which gives you the benefit of shelter, a little comfort, and a good view, while also reducing disturbance to the local bird population. Ducks and other shorebirds at the water's edge are prone to fly off and never return, so keeping still and watching from a fixed point can be particularly important here.

Out on the water, you may see grebes, cormorants, and a variety of ducks, usually grouped into diving ducks and surface feeders (or "dabbling" ducks). Some dabblers, such as wigeon, also feed on adjacent grassland and often rest on the bank. In winter, both number and variety are greatly increased. Start at one end and scan through the flocks to see what you can find. Lakes may serve as nighttime roosts for thousands of gulls, especially in winter. Even when these water habitats are far inland, if the water levels are low, migrant waders such as greater and lesser yellowlegs, dowitchers, dunlins, and semipalmated plovers will be attracted to them, especially in spring and fall.

Expert fisher
In summer, keep an eye on the skies over the water for an osprey hunting for fish.

At the water's edge
With greenish-yellow legs and a speckled back, a solitary sandpiper may be seen on the shore.

Scooping up food
On the water, the northern shoveler's broad bill is adapted to sieve food from near the water's surface.

Rites of courtship
Clark's grebes perform their ritualized mating "dance" in spring, displaying their red eyes and saberlike bills. They may pass nesting material to one another.

REDHEAD
17–21 in

This medium-sized diving duck drifts along by day, foraging mainly around dawn and dusk. The redhead often lays its eggs in other duck nests.

Breeding male has a black and white crested head

♀

Male has a brick-red head and neck

HOODED MERGANSER
15½–19½ in

This merganser can raise and lower its crest during courtship displays. It is a cavity nester and may use a nest box close to water.

♀

Tall, pointed head

RING-NECKED DUCK
15–18 in

Despite this duck's name, the chestnut ring around its neck is hard to see. This medium-sized diving duck can take flight by leaping directly from the water.

Breeding male has iridescent green head

♀

COMMON GOLDENEYE
15½–20 in

Aggressive with other cavity nesters, including its own species, this midsized, compact diving duck often lays eggs in other duck nests. Its wings whir in flight.

Shovel-like bill for feeding on water surface

NORTHERN SHOVELER
17⅓–20 in

A large, heavy-headed dabbling duck, the shoveler "sweeps" its bill through the water to feed on plant matter and invertebrates.

♀

Green patch on hind wings

GREEN-WINGED TEAL
12–15½ in

The smallest North American dabbling duck, this teal prefers shallow lakes with abundant standing vegetation. It often rests out of water.

White cheek on nonbreeding adult

Breeding birds have a gold band

HORNED GREBE
12–15 in

This grebe's "horns" are yellowish feathers behind its eyes that can be raised at will. In flight, its head and neck are aligned with the body.

Distinct white diamond on hindwing

♀

GADWALL
18–22⅓ in

More commonly spotted in winter, this large dabbling duck is relatively plain, but both male and female have a white patch on the wing.

Birds of lakes, reservoirs, and gravel pits

Many landbirds are drawn to drink from, or feed over and around lakes, while "edge" habitats such as shoreline pebbles, mud or grass, and reeds and willow thickets, all add variety for waterbirds.

PURPLE MARTIN
7–8 in

The largest of all North American swallows, the purple martin is often found near water. It performs aerial acrobatics as it catches insects.

Brown-black tail

Brown above with a black collar

KILLDEER
8–11 in

This shorebird's piercing "dee-ee" call carries for long distances. A vigilant parent, the killdeer sometimes feigns a broken wing to distract predators from its chicks.

GREAT EGRET
37–41 in

Preferring to forage alone, the great egret maintains a territory about 10 feet in diameter around itself as it moves around and feeds.

Watch from a blind to see a wide range of birds going about their daily life

OSPREY
21⅓–22¾ in

Perched high on a branch over the water, or hovering and diving for fish, this large raptor is an impressive sight.

Black stripe behind eye

Dark brown upper parts and white underparts

BLACK TERN
9–14¼ in

In the summer, this small, elegant tern has a black head and belly, with gray wings. It typically flies low over the water to catch insects.

Black stripe on bill

Hooked bill

Long neck

PIED-BILLED GREBE
11¾–15 in

This wide-ranging grebe can migrate over 2,000 miles. Pairs duet during mating season. It breeds on lakes and ponds, even in populated areas.

DOUBLE-CRESTED CORMORANT
28–35 in

The cormorant builds its nest of sticks and grass in a colony near small lagoons. As well as providing food, the parent bird brings its chicks water in its bill, and uses its body to provide shade.

Lark song
Meadowlarks sing a sweet, whistling tune over fields to proclaim their nesting territory and to attract a mate.

Farmland, hedgerows, and grassland

The birds you see in this habitat will vary with the seasons and the rhythms of the farming calendar. Much depends too on local farming practices, which may leave bird populations vulnerable.

Adapting to change

By its very nature, farmland changes through the year, as seeds are spread, grass is cut, and crops are harvested. But birds have had to adjust to changes in farming practices, which have had a significant impact. Some farmland species have declined enormously, such as meadowlarks, grasshopper sparrows, and bobolinks. Winter flocks—a once frequent sight—are also diminished, so you're less likely to see mixed flocks of horned larks, longspurs, and snow buntings. Grassland birds have declined in part because the prairies that once covered much of North America were converted to farmland; the mowing of hay fields too early in the spring destroys the nests of ground-nesting birds.

There is still much to see in farmland habitats, however, especially if hedges have been retained and wildlife-friendly farming practices are in use. Look for gulls following the plow on arable land, and pheasants, turkeys, and geese patrolling the fields for seeds, grains, and grasses. Flocks of red-winged blackbirds and grackles invade early-winter hedgerows and close-cropped pastures, with northern harriers hovering overhead. An isolated old oak is a good place to find a red-tailed hawk—but you must find a rough, unimproved grassy meadow to hope for a hunting barn owl.

Nesting on the ground
Bobolinks often nest on the ground in hay fields, but when the fields are cut too early or too often, it destroys their nests.

Turning up worms
Large flocks of mixed gulls follow the plow as it turns over the soil and offers up worms for them to eat.

In the hedges
Cedar waxwings thrive on small red fruits; they benefit the shrubs that produce these fruits by dispersing seeds.

Birds of farmland, hedgerows, and grassland

Although numbers have decreased in recent decades, there's still a variety of birdlife, often feeding on seeds and insects, or predating the smaller mammals sharing the space.

Thick bill

AMERICAN CROW
15¾–21 in

Common across North America, the American Crow gathers in large flocks to forage on agricultural fields. It eats grains, seeds, and insects, including some crop pests.

Black overall

MOURNING DOVE
9–13½ in

Perched on a telephone wire, wooden post, or branch, the mourning dove sings a soft, melancholy song.

Soft brown overall; black wing spots

Iridescent neck feathers

Male is bright red overall; female tan with red accents

ROCK PIGEON
11¾–14¼ in

This familiar bird finds nesting sites in barns and grain towers. It builds its nest from straw and other plant materials.

NORTHERN CARDINAL
8–9 in

Cardinals are a familiar sight in the east, especially in fields and hedgerows. They sing a loud, whistled "cheer, cheer, cheer."

Rufous shoulders

Breeding male has blue body; female brown overall

KILLDEER
8–11 in

When vegetation is low, the killdeer can be spotted walking or running in short bursts across grasslands as it searches for earthworms.

INDIGO BUNTING
5½ in

Once dependent on forest edges, this brilliant blue songbird now prefers to breed in disturbed fields.

DICKCISSEL
5½–6⅓ in

A tallgrass prairie specialist, this bird rarely breeds outside of this range. In winter, it is often mistaken for a sparrow.

RING-NECKED PHEASANT
19½–28 in

This pheasant, introduced to North America for hunting purposes, is now widespread. It is easiest to spot in open fields, especially after harvest.

Breeding male has black hood and back

EASTERN TOWHEE
6–8¼ in

Known for its distinctive feeding style, this towhee jumps backward with both feet to move leaves, exposing the insects and seeds underneath.

Black eyes set in white face

BARN OWL
12⅔–15¾ in

At dawn or dusk, you may see this medium-sized owl out on the prowl, flying low in search of prey. It has a white front and golden-sandy back.

SHORT-EARED OWL
13½–16 in

This medium-sized owl builds its nest by scraping a hole in the ground that is concealed by vegetation. It then lines the nest with grass and feathers.

NORTHERN HARRIER
18–20 in

The northern harrier flies low over open fields in search of mice and voles. Unusually for a hawk, it relies on its hearing to find prey.

Long tail

White barred underwings

NORTHERN BOBWHITE
8–10 in

A small, plump bird, this quail is named for its cheerful "bob WHITE" call, whistled by breeding males. When startled, it erupts in a small flock.

Black bill, head and neck

CANADA GOOSE
30–43⅓ in

This large waterbird grazes in farm fields where it feeds on grasses in spring, and grain in winter.

Black legs and feet

RING-BILLED GULL
17–21½ in

Flocking around fields, this opportunistic feeder searches for insects, worms, and grain. It can be seen walking on the ground or hovering in the air.

Yellow legs; pink in juveniles

VESPER SPARROW
5–6¼ in

Named for its sweet evening song, the vesper sparrow needs bare ground to breed and forages in fields and other open grassy areas.

Pale brown upperparts

SAVANNAH SPARROW
4½–6 in

Across its vast range, this sparrow shows wide variation. However, all are brown with dark streaks above and white with dark streaks below.

Yellow stripe over eye

Forests and woodlands

What you see birdwatching in forests depends on the season and place but also the types of trees growing there. You will hear a lot more than you see, so listen and watch carefully.

Hiding and watching

Forest birdwatching can be frustrating: you'll hear lots of birds, but they're often hidden by foliage, so you won't see as many as you hear. In late summer, even the best woods might seem empty, as birds wander in flocks or hide during their annual molt. Which birds you'll encounter depends on the time of year and geographical location, but also the species and density of trees growing in the forest.

Conifers have specialists such as crossbills, and adaptable birds such as hairy woodpeckers, and localized species such as boreal chickadees might appear. A conifer within a deciduous wood can attract the local black-capped chickadees and golden-crowned kinglets. Old deciduous trees have familiar birds such as red-eyes vireos, scarlet tanagers, and wood thrush. You may also see less common species such as great crested flycatchers, cerulean warblers, and American redstarts. Western coastal forests may be home to varied thrush, Townsend's warblers, Canada jays, and northern spotted owls.

In late summer and fall, the migration of most forest birds begins. Warblers, vireos, and flycatchers migrate from northern forests to their winter homes, often in South America. At this time of year, don't forget to look up for a sight of migrating predators, such as buteos, accipiters, and falcons.

On tree trunks
You may hear a pileated woodpecker before you see it, hunting for food under tree bark or chiseling out a nest hole.

Conifer specialist
On conifers, see red crossbills, which have crossed bill tips and a thick tongue to help pry open cones and extract seeds.

Irruptive migrators
Pine siskins migrate when there are shortages of conifer seeds in northern forests. Their tiny beaks extract seeds from pine cones.

In the trees
Barred owls frequent moist lowland forests, especially those with large trees where they may find cavities spacious enough to raise a family.

RED-EYED VIREO
6 in

This vireo's persistent three-note song, emanating from deciduous forest canopies, is a familiar summer sound.

Black necklace

Wings and tail have black bars

BLUE JAY
9¼–12 in

This songbird calls from its tree perch on the edge of forests. It is especially fond of acorns and can be found near oak trees.

Yellow-orange crown patch

Male has red cheek stripe

GOLDEN-CROWNED KINGLET
3¼–4¼ in

This tiny bird breeds in northern mountainous conifer forests. Midwestern spruce tree planting has increased its breeding range.

PILEATED WOODPECKER
15¾–19⅓ in

The largest North American woodpecker, it is easily recognized by its scarlet crest and loud, laughlike "yuk yuk yuk" call.

Black streaks on back and chest

BARRED OWL
17–19½ in

Mostly nocturnal, the barred owl may also hunt or call by day. Its distinctive hooting call sounds like "who cooks for you?"

YELLOW-RUMPED WARBLER
4⅗–5½ in

Eastern and western forms of this bird can interbreed. Their ability to winter in a variety of habitats has made these warblers widespread.

Boldly striped underparts

Dark eyes and yellow bill

COOPER'S HAWK
14⅗–17¾ in

An incredible, skillful flier, this hawk can maneuver quickly through dense vegetation as it preys on other birds.

AMERICAN GOSHAWK
21–25¼ in

Although secretive by nature, the American goshawk fiercely defends its territory, nest, and chicks, fending off intruders, including humans, with a loud, high-pitched "gek gek gek."

Birds of forests and woodlands

Birds can be hard to spot in the depths of a forest, since they have to be alert and hide from phenomenal predators such as the "phantom of the forest," the American goshawk.

Black and white head stripes

RED-BREASTED NUTHATCH
4¼ in

Recognizable by its distinctive black eye-stripe and nasal one-note "ank" call, this inquisitive nuthatch breeds in coniferous forests.

Plump body with orange-buff underparts

AMERICAN WOODCOCK
9¾–12¼ in

Woodcocks are nocturnal and seldom seen, except during their unique springtime courtship displays. The male's wings twitter during display flights, followed by a nasal "peent" upon landing.

Mottled brown above

BROWN CREEPER
5¼ in

With soft calls and cryptic plumage, this creeper is easily overlooked. When foraging, it climbs up a tree trunk, flies down, then starts up another tree.

Male has an often-concealed red patch on crown

RUBY-CROWNED KINGLET
3½–4⅓ in

Known for its loud, complex song and incessant wing-flicking, this tiny bird can lay up to 12 eggs per clutch.

Crossed mandibles

RED CROSSBILL
5¼–6⅓ in

A highly adapted bill enables the crossbill to pry apart the scales of conifer cones; the conifer seed is then lifted out with the tongue.

Be patient, watch, and listen for tell-tale signs such as a branch jiggling or movement on a tree trunk

White cheeks and breast

BLACK-CAPPED CHICKADEE
4¾–5¾ in

This acrobatic little chickadee is often seen in a flock or with other small birds, including warblers and vireos. It nests in cavities within birch and alder trees.

Small, round bill

TUFTED TITMOUSE
5½–6⅓ in

Commonly found in deciduous and evergreen forests in the east, the tufted titmouse forages for seeds, nuts, and insects.

Female has olive-yellow upperparts

Male has scarlet head and body

SCARLET TANAGER
6¼–6¾ in

The breeding male tanager is one of North America's most easily identified birds. But its elusive nature and preference for well-shaded forest canopies make it hard to find.

Streaked underparts and back

PINE SISKIN
4¼–5½ in

Twittering incessantly, this energetic conifer dweller zips over trees in small flocks in search of seeds and insects.

Prickly habitat
Pyrrhuloxia can be distinguished from Northern Cardinals by their yellow bill and mostly gray plumage. And, unlike cardinals, they nest among prickly pear cactuses in dry desert habitats.

Deserts and dry shrublands

The cactus, agave, and mesquite that thrive in desert and dry shrubland environments create secure nesting places, shelter from intense sun, and abundant food for a unique community of birds.

Big skies and broad landscapes

Deserts might at first seem like lifeless places, but this is an illusion, and many species of birds are only found here. In a habitat largely devoid of trees, giant cactuses may be the tallest plants in an otherwise broad, open landscape. Desert birding is best in the early morning, at dusk, and at night. During daylight hours, greater road runners, cactus wrens, Gambel's quail, and verdin can be seen in rocky canyons and along dry streambeds where desert plants such as mesquite and yucca thrive. Here, chuparosa and fairy duster shrubs produce colorful flowers that sustain tiny Costa's hummingbirds. At night, temperatures can plummet, but this is the ideal time for nocturnal birds such as common poorwills, elf owls, and lesser nighthawks to come out to hunt.

Deserts and dry (xeric) shrublands make up the largest biome on Earth, covering 19 percent of the planet's land surface. Xeric habitats, by definition, receive less than 10 inches of rain per year. Here, some plants lie dormant in summer but bloom and fruit in fall and winter with increased rain. These conditions favor low-growing shrubs with leathery leaves such as honey mesquite, toyon, and lemonade berry. These plants offer excellent cover, nesting places, and food for scrub-jays, curve-billed thrashers, and white-winged doves.

Frequent feeder
A Costa's hummingbird visits an estimated 1,840 flowers daily to meet its energy needs.

Grouping together
The plump Gambel's quail forages in groups called coveys and prefers running to flying.

Standing out
While coastal populations of the California scrub-jay are easily seen, they can be elusive inland.

GREATER ROADRUNNER
21 in

As their name implies, this roadrunner prefers running to flying. Its speed allows it to chase down and capture small birds and lizards on foot.

Very long, dark tail

PHAINOPEPLA
7–8⅓ in

The phainopepla breeds in winter and again in summer. It feeds on fruit, especially desert mistletoe, and catches flying insects from its treetop perches.

PYRRHULOXIA
8⅓ in

Pyrrhuloxia can be distinguished from northern cardinals by its yellow bill and mostly gray plumage. It is most at home in dry desert habitats, where it nests among prickly pear cacti.

Gray plumage with red accents

COMMON POORWILL
7½–8⅓ in

This nocturnal bird whistles "Poor wheelup!" at night. During cold weather when food is scarce, it can go into a state of torpor for several weeks.

Mottled brownish gray plumage; white throat band

Blue skin around orange eyes

WHITE-WINGED DOVE
11⅓ in

Unlike most doves, the white-winged dove makes its home in semiarid habitats. It flashes white wing bands in flight.

Plump body; chestnut sides

Black forward-facing top knot

GAMBEL'S QUAIL
11 in

This ground bird forages in thorny, shrubby areas within the southwestern desert. It prefers running to flying but explodes into flight when startled.

Plan desert birding for dawn and dusk, when temperatures are more comfortable

BLACK-THROATED SPARROW
5¼ in

This sparrow's tinkling call notes may be heard in barren creosote brush of the southwest.

Black throat and mask

Blue wings; long blue tail

Gray underparts

WOODHOUSE'S SCRUB JAY
11–12 in

This jay, found in the dry open habitats of the west, is elusive; you are more likely to hear its harsh call than see it. It is a lively bird, making hops and lunges as it moves around.

Violet crown and throat patch

Greenish sides

COSTA'S HUMMINGBIRD
3¼ in

This small hummingbird can be found in desert scrubland, where it feeds on the nectar of flowering chuparosa and ocotillo plants.

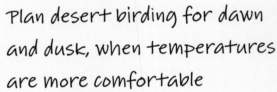

Birds of deserts and dry shrublands

Desert birds are adaptable and often as unique as the land in which they live. Common poorwills are known to enter a torpid state; greater roadrunners can secrete excess salt.

White eyebrows

ELF OWL
4¾–5½ in

The world's smallest owl, the elf owl is also a common raptor in the southwestern desert. It has distinctive chattering calls.

Dusty gray back; brown-spotted white underparts

CURVE-BILLED THRASHER
10⅔–11 in

This thrasher's two-note "twit twit" call is common in southwestern semi-deserts. Its curved bill is useful in foraging for ground insects.

GILDED FLICKER
11–11½ in

The gilded flicker typically excavates its nest inside a saguaro cactus, which helps protect its chicks from predators.

Golden yellow underwings

Yellow body and head

Brown cap; white eyebrows

CACTUS WREN
7–8¾ in

This wren sings repeatedly from cactus tops and nests within cacti in southwestern deserts.

HOODED ORIOLE
7–8 in

This oriole lives in deserts with sycamores and cottonwoods, but it has also taken to nesting in suburban California's tall palm trees.

Yellow head; gray back

VERDIN
3½–4⅓ in

Verdins are constantly flitting about within their low-elevation southwestern desert habitat. They often drink flower nectar.

HARRIS'S HAWK
18–23 in

Unlike other North American hawks, Harris's hawks nest and hunt in groups; they take turns leading the hunt to tire out the prey, then share the meat.

Rufous shoulders; dark brown upperparts, chest, and belly

Orange nape

GOLDEN-FRONTED WOODPECKER
8¾–10¼ in

Besides this bird's yellow forehead, the white rump patch in flight and the male's red crown are prominent features. It has a loud, laughing call.

Black and white barred upperparts

147

Mountains and foothills

Birdlife changes with elevation on foothills and mountains. There are fewer species here than in other habitats, but they find a way to live in this wild terrain.

A harsh, beautiful environment

The foothills and low shoulders of mountains are often covered in conifers that then blend into rocky hills and peaks as the altitude increases and the treeline recedes. Birds are generally few in number and variety here, and those who make a home on rocky peaks and crags are different from the birds living at lower elevations.

Above the treeline is rough grass, often with wet, boggy valleys and scattered shrubs. Look for ravens and ptarmigan above the tree line, and American pipits almost everywhere, which in turn attract merlins, a bird-eating falcon. Deep gullies and crags may have rosy finches, and patches of smooth grass close by are good for northern wheatears. In foothills, Vaux's swifts usually nest in hollow coniferous trees; white-throated swifts attach their nests to rocky cliffs and catch tiny insects overhead.

If you're going higher, prepare for the weather and conditions. Look for ravens and, if you are in an area where there are golden eagles, scan the skyline, even at a great distance. A big brown bird of prey close up is likely to be a red-tailed hawk, but a distant dot could be an eagle—and, who knows, it may come closer.

Perched high
In spring, look on cliff ledges and in tall trees to see the nest of a raven, a huge corvid that behaves like a bird of prey.

In the mountains
In summer, try to see the red-naped sapsucker, which lives at lower elevations on western mountains.

On the rocks
A resident of the highest peaks, the ptarmigan has white wings and turns almost completely white in winter.

Apex predator
The mountains are golden eagle territory. Their eyes are so keen that they can spot a rodent miles below.

Birds of mountains and foothills

Unforgiving in winter, uplands in spring can become much busier as birds head to high elevations to breed. Few species are entirely mountain birds, but some are characteristic of upland areas.

Golden head; darker on juveniles

Dark-brown upperparts fade in summer

GOLDEN EAGLE
26–39⅓ in

Huge and long-tailed, the golden eagle soars on broad, raised wings. Often at a great height, this magnificent bird of prey hunts over lowland valleys and high peaks.

Large yellow feet have hooked black claws

Black wings with white wing patches and gray body

CLARKE'S NUTCRACKER
10⅔–11¾ in

Named for its ability to extract pine nuts with its strong bill, this bird caches nuts when they are abundant and solicits food from human visitors.

STELLER'S JAY
11–12 in

In western coniferous forests, this dark jay can disappear into the shadows. An inquisitive bird, it also frequents campgrounds.

Deep blue lower body and black upper half

Females gray-brown with blue wings

MERLIN
9⅓–13 in

Floating on the breeze or flying fast and low, the merlin is a small, dynamic falcon of upland slopes and wooded gullies.

Male is blue-gray above; female is brown

Males are bright blue overall

MOUNTAIN BLUEBIRD
6–8 in

This western bluebird feeds by hovering over subalpine meadows then pouncing on insects below. Males guard their mates until egg-hatching time.

MOUNTAIN CHICKADEE
5½ in

Named for its high elevation habitat, this bird stores seeds in preparation for cold winters. To avoid pilfering, it stores food caches further away when other chickadees are nearby.

Male has ruby red throat patch

Long, straight bill

Long tail feathers

BROAD-TAILED HUMMINGBIRD
4 in

This hummingbird may arrive at alpine meadows to breed before the snow melts. Until flowers bloom, it survives on insects and tree sap from holes drilled by red-naped sapsuckers.

Red throat and crown

RED-NAPED SAPSUCKER
8–9 in

Named for its ability to drink tree sap with its specialized tongue, it drills holes in rows on trees in high-altitude forests and eats insects that are attracted by the sweet sap.

Hike up in spring to listen to the songs of birds making their nests in this rugged wilderness

Black overall

White crescents between eyes

GREAT GRAY OWL
24–33 in

North America's tallest owl, the great gray can plunge through deep snow to snatch prey, detected by sound.

COMMON RAVEN
22–27¼ in

Found in both foothills and deep mountain forests, this large raven can be heard making a croaking call.

Long black tail feathers

Streaked underparts

Fanned tail

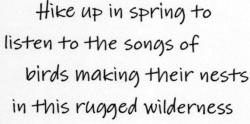
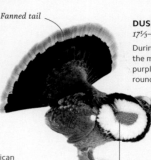

DUSKY GROUSE
17⅓–22½ in

During ground-based courtship displays, the male dusky grouse shows red or purple air sacs on its neck and fans out its rounded black tail to impress females.

GREATER SAGE-GROUSE
22–29½ in

By far the largest North American grouse, males gather in large groups called leks, where they perform spectacular courtship displays to impress the females.

Red air sacs on side of neck

Snow white in winter

Brown in summer

Male has white breast and neck

Dark mottled plumage

ROCK PTARMIGAN
12⅔–15¾ in

With a small head and a plump body, the rock ptarmigan's winter plumage blends in with its snowy surroundings. Feathered feet help it stay on top of the snow.

Glossary

Adult A fully mature bird that is able to breed and usually in its final plumage.

Altricial A young bird that is helpless and dependent on its parents when it hatches.

Barred With marks that cross the body, wings, or tail.

Bird of prey A predatory carnivorous bird with acute eyesight, muscular legs, and sharp bill and talons.

Breeding plumage The plumage worn when birds display and pair.

Brood Young produced from a single clutch of eggs that are incubated together.

Call Vocal sound conveying a variety of messages, often particular to a single species.

Churring A repetitive trill, such as that produced by young woodpeckers in the nest.

Clutch A group of eggs laid in a single nest, and incubated together.

Colony A group of the same species nesting together.

Covert A small feather in a well-defined tract on the wing or at the base of the tail, covering the base of larger flight feathers.

Dabble To feed in shallow water by filtering water through the bill to remove food such as seeds, hence "dabbling duck."

Dawn chorus The short-lived concentration of birdsong around dawn, especially in spring.

Display Ritualized behavior often used in courtship, to claim territory, or (as a distraction display) to lure a predator away from a nest.

Diving duck A species of duck that swims on the surface, from which it dives under to seek food.

Drumming An instrumental sound made by vibrating the bill against a branch (as in woodpeckers) or vibrating outspread tail feathers through the air (as in Wilson's snipe).

Ear tuft A bunch of feathers on an owl's head that can be raised as a visual signal.

Eclipse Summer plumage of ducks and some other species, to help camouflage them during their molt.

Eyebrow A line of color above the eye and cheek (can also be known as a superciliary stripe).

Eye patch An area of color around the eye.

Eye ring A ring of color around the eye.

Eyestripe A stripe of color running in front of and behind the eye.

Feral Living wild, but derived from domestic stock that has escaped.

Fledge To leave the nest or acquire the first complete set of flight feathers. Birds that do this are known as fledglings.

Flight feathers A collective term for the large feathers on a bird's wing (primaries and secondaries).

Forewing The front part of the spread wing, including outer primaries, primary coverts, and smaller secondary coverts.

Immature Not yet fully adult or generally able to breed.

Incubate To keep eggs warm as they develop, until they hatch.

Inner wing The inner half of the wing, including the secondary coverts and secondaries.

Juvenile A bird in its first plumage, before it has its first molt.

Lek A gathering of birds at which the males display or fight to impress watching females before mating (without forming pairs).

Migrant A species that spends part of the year in one geographical area and part in another, "migrating" between the two.

Molt The shedding of old feathers and growth of new replacements in a systematic fashion that is characteristic of the species.

Mottled Flecked with patches of color.

Moustache A stripe of colored feather extending from the base of the bill.

Orbital ring A thin, bare, fleshy ring around the eye, often of a distinctive color.

Outer wing The outer half of the spread wing, including the primaries and primary coverts.

Plunge-diving Diving into water from the air, rather than a perch or the surface, to catch a fish.

Precocial A young bird that is well developed at hatching and soon able to fend for itself.

Preening Maintaining the feathers in good condition by cleaning, smoothing, oiling, and lubricating them.

Primary One of the large outer wing feathers, growing from the digits.

Roost A place where birds sleep, or the act of sleeping.

Scapular One of a more or less oval tract of feathers growing from the shoulders, each side of the back.

Secondary One of the row of long, stiff feathers at the trailing edge of the inner wing.

Shorebird A bird or species within a group of families, including plovers and sandpipers, that live near water.

Song A vocal performance with a pattern characteristic of the species; may attract a mate, or repel intruders from a territory.

Song-flight A special and usually distinctive flight in which the song is performed; often short (as in warblers), but sometimes prolonged (as in larks).

Species A group of living organisms, individuals of which can interbreed and produce fertile offspring, but which usually do not or cannot breed with individuals of other species.

Streaked Marked with lines of color aligned lengthwise along the body.

Subspecies A more or less distinct group within a species, defined by geographical area; also "race."

Superciliary stripe A line of color above the eye (also called the eyebrow).

Tail coverts (upper and under) Feathers covering the base of the tail.

Talon The claw of a bird of prey.

Tarsus The longest, most obvious part of a bird's leg, between the "toes" and the "ankle joint" (often called the "knee," but points backward).

Territory An area defended by a pair or individual, for breeding or feeding.

Tertial One of a small group of feathers at the base of the wing, adjacent to the innermost secondaries.

Waterfowl A loose term that includes wildfowl, rails, wading birds, and grebes.

Wildfowl A collective term specifically for ducks, geese, and swans.

Wing bar A line of color across the coverts on the closed wing, or along the extended wing as a bar or stripe.

Next steps

USEFUL WEBSITES

On these websites, you can find further information on birdwatching, sites to visit, local clubs to join, and much more.

National Audubon Society One of the oldest bird conservation organizations, the Audubon Society works to protect birds and their habitats. It also carries out scientific research. *www.audubon.org*

Cornell Laboratory of Ornithology The laboratory conducts scientific research, citizen science initiatives, and provides education. It has an online guide to birds and birdwatching called *All About Birds*, and a photography collection, the Macaulay Library, that is useful for identification. *www.birds.cornell.edu*

The Nature Conservancy A global environmental organization concerned with climate change and biodiversity loss. They have a network of nature preserves that are open to visitors. *www.nature.org*

National Wildlife Federation The federation is a conservation organization that aims to educate on the conservation of wildlife and their habitats. *www.nwf.org*

American Bird Conservancy An organization for the conservation of birds and their habitats. Its website has a useful online library of bird profiles. *www.abcbirds.org*

American Birding Association An organization that provides encouragement and educational resources for the birdwatching community as well as helping to protect birds. Its website has resources for birders. *www.aba.org*

The American Ornithological Society A network for ornithologists that advocates for the study and conservation of birds. *www.americanornithology.org*

BirdLife International A global collaboration of organizations that works to conserve birds and their habitats. Its website holds a huge amount of information on species' range and status. *www.birdlife.org*

Flock Together A birdwatching organization for people of color. *www.flocktogether.world*

Fatbirder Information about birdwatching worldwide. *www.fatbirder.com*

Xeno Canto A comprehensive collection of bird recordings. *www.xeno-canto.org*

Project MartinWatch A citizen science project to track the reproduction of purple martins. *www.purplemartin.org/research*

USEFUL READING

Here are some other DK books you might find interesting and helpful.

American Museum of Natural History Birds of North America

Pocket Birds of North America: Eastern Region

Pocket Birds of North America: Western Region

What's that Bird?

How to Attract Birds to Your Garden

Bird: The Definitive Visual Guide

The Bird Book

USEFUL APPS

These are just some of the many apps available to help you identify the birds around you, via sound or image.

Merlin Bird ID	iBird Pro
BirdNET	eBird
ChirpOMatic	Seek
BirdID	iNaturalist

Index

Page numbers in **bold** refer to main entries

Acknowledgments

DK would like to thank Noor Ali for design assistance; Helen Peters for the index; and Michelle Harris, Michaela Weglinski, and Katie John for fact-checking. Picture research: Ridhima Sikka, Vagisha Pushp. Jacket designer: Rhea Menon. DTP designer: Rakesh Kumar. Senior jackets coordinator: Priyanka Sharma Saddi. Jackets design development manager: Sophia MTT.

From the first UK edition:
Editor: Stephanie Farrow
Illustrators: Phil Gamble, Ali Scrivens

The name of the Smithsonian Institution and the sunburst logo are registered trademarks of the Smithsonian Institution. For more information, please visit www.si.edu

Picture credits

The publisher would like to thank the following for their kind permission to reproduce their photographs:

(Key: a-above; b-below/bottom; c-center; f-far; l-left; r-right; t-top)

1 Getty Images: Johner Images. **2 Shutterstock.com:** Puffin's Pictures. **6-7 Shutterstock.com:** Agami Photo Agency. **10 Getty Images / iStock:** E+ / Goodboy Picture Company. **11 Getty Images:** Westend61 (br). **12 Dreamstime.com:** Elena Goosen (crb). **12-13 Alamy Stock Photo:** Zbynek Pospisil. **14-15 Alamy Stock Photo:** Allen Creative / Steve Allen (t). **15 Alamy Stock Photo:** David Burton (br). **17 Getty Images:** Universal Images Group / Education Images. **18 Alamy Stock Photo:** TravelMuse (br). **19 Alamy Stock Photo:** ARV (crb); TravelMuse (tr); Chris Howarth / Iceland (bl). **21 Getty Images:** Moment / Nitat Termmee (tr). **22-23 Getty Images:** Mint Images - Oliver Edwards. **26-27 Getty Images:** Associated Press / David Duprey (b). **28 Getty Images:** Moment / Massimo Ravera (cra); Westend61 (b). **30-31 ©Chris Packham:** (x3). **32 ©Chris Packham:** (x3). **33 Alamy Stock Photo:** David Stuckel (cra). **Dreamstime.com:** Robert Adami (clb). **Getty Images / iStock:** blightylad-infocus (tr). **35 Getty Images / iStock:** E+ / PamelaJoeMcFarlane. **36 Getty Images / iStock:** KAMPUS. **37 Getty Images / iStock:** E+ / StefaNikolic. **38 Dreamstime.com:** Donnaallard (clb). **39 Dreamstime.com:** Yuri Arcurs. **42-43 Dreamstime.com:** Eniko Balogh. **43 Getty Images:** Moment / Stan Tekiela Author / Naturalist / Wildlife Photographer (cla). **Shutterstock.com:** Whytock (cra). **45 Depositphotos Inc:** steve_byland (bl). Dorling Kindersley: Chris Gomersall Photography (tl); Mike Lane (tr); Robert Royse (br). **Dreamstime.com:** Rck953 (cr). **Shutterstock.com:** Ihor Hvozdetskyi (cl); Annette Shaff (bc). **46 Alamy Stock Photo:** Science Photo Library / Steve Gschmeissner (br). **46-47 Dreamstime.com:** Aline Bedard. **47 Shutterstock.com:** Chase D'animulls (crb). **48 Alamy Stock Photo:** imageBROKER.com GmbH & Co. KG / C. Huetter (br). **Dorling Kindersley:** Alan Murphy (bl). **Shutterstock.com:** anitapol (feathers). **49 Alamy Stock Photo:** Robert Garrigus (cra/red-shafted); Christian Hütter (owl wing); Nick Greaves; Agfa Awards Winner (cr); imageBROKER.com GmbH & Co. KG / Erhard Nerger (crb); Naturepix (bl). **Dorling Kindersley:** Barnabas Kindersley (tl). **Dreamstime.com:** Melinda Fawver (cla, cla/jay tail); Natallia Yaumenenka (tr); Stefan Schug (cra/flicker). **Getty Images / iStock:** E+ / Gregory_DUBUS (b); Krzysztof12 (c); epantha (crb/Woodpecker). **Shutterstock.com:** Gallinago_media (cra). **50-51 Alamy Stock Photo:** Richard Mittleman / Gon2Foto. **51 Alamy Stock Photo:** Stobbe (tl). **Shutterstock.com:** onewildlifer (tr). **52 Getty Images:** Moment / Javier Fernández Sánchez. **53 Alamy Stock Photo:** Robert Kennett (crb). **Dreamstime.com:** Sue Feldberg (tr); Wirestock (tl). **54 Alamy Stock Photo:** AGAMI Photo Agency / Ralph Martin (clb); Parmorama (cla); Nature Photographers Ltd / Paul R. Sterry (br). **55 Alamy Stock Photo:** AGAMI Photo Agency / Ralph Martin (b); Janice and Nolan Braud (tl); EB Photography (cra). **56 Alamy Stock Photo:** Nature Picture Library / Rolf Nussbaumer (crb); Johann Schumacher (cra). **Getty Images:** Moment / Jeff R Clow. **58 Dreamstime.com:** Anagram1 (cr); Dgareri (c); Tobie1953 (cl); Paul Reeves (c/Scythe); Alexander Potapov (bc); Wildphotos (br). **59 Alamy Stock Photo:** imageBROKER.com GmbH & Co. KG / Dave Pressland (cr). **Dorling Kindersley:** David Cottridge (c). **Dreamstime.com:** Gerald Deboer (bc); Isselee (cla, cl). **Getty Images:** Sharif Uddin / 500px (br); Universal Images Group / Education Images (ca). **Getty Images / iStock:** studio-laska (bl). **Shutterstock.com:** John L. Absher (bc/Flycatcher). **60 Shutterstock.com:** scooperdigital (bl). **61 Alamy Stock Photo:** Guy Bell (crb). **Getty Images / iStock:** Ken Griffiths (tr). **63 Getty Images:** The Image Bank / Hal Beral. **64 Dreamstime.com:** Rudmer Zwerver (crb). **65 naturepl.com:** David Pattyn. **66 Alamy Stock Photo:** Arterra Picture Library / Arndt Sven-Erik (t). **Shutterstock.com:** Ryan Noeker (b). **67 Getty Images:** Moment / Cyrielle Beaubois. **68 Alamy Stock Photo:** Tom Reichner. **69 Alamy Stock Photo:** Arterra Picture Library / Arndt Sven-Erik. **70 Alamy Stock Photo:** All Canada Photos / Grambo Photography (bc); Mike O'Carroll (bl); Minden Pictures / Scott Leslie (br). **71 Getty Images:** Dario Pautasso / 500px. **72 Getty Images:** Judy Tomlinson / 500px. **73 Dreamstime.com:** Rck953 (tc). **Getty Images / iStock:** E+ / lavin photography (cr). **Shutterstock.com:** Jennifer Bosvert (tr); James W. Thompson (cl); Paul Tessier (c). **74-75 Alamy Stock Photo:** Kit Day (b). **75 Alamy Stock Photo:** Sue Phillips (tc). **Dreamstime.com:** Vlad Ghiea (tl). **Getty Images / iStock:** Aaron Seltzer (tr). **76 Alamy Stock Photo:** Jess Merrill (bc); Westend61 GmbH / Fotofeeling (bl); Nature Picture Library / David Tipling (br). **77 Shutterstock.com:** Jeanne Crockett. **78 Shutterstock.com:** PJ photography. **79 Alamy Stock Photo:** Ross Knowlton Nature Photography. **80 Alamy Stock Photo:** Richardom (bl). **Shutterstock.com:** Mark Caunt (br). **81 Alamy Stock Photo:** David Tipling Photo Library (tr); Ivan Kuzmin (b). **82 Alamy Stock Photo:** Arterra Picture Library / Arndt Sven-Erik. **84 Alamy Stock Photo:** blickwinkel / Hecker (br). **Dreamstime.com:** Cristianzamfir (bl); Xalanx (bc). **85 Alamy Stock Photo:** Jim Clark (br); Realimage (t); Tommi Syvänperä (bc). **Getty Images / iStock:** Heather Jon Photography (b). **88-89 Dreamstime.com:** Melodyanne (b). **89 Shutterstock.com:** Alexander Sviridov (cra). **90 Dreamstime.com:** Le Thuy Do (tr). **Getty Images:** Jack Borno / 500px (tl). **91 Alamy Stock Photo:** Jill Morgan (cr). **Getty Images / iStock:** E+ / lleerogers (tc). **92 Alamy Stock Photo:** Arterra Picture Library / De Meester Johan. **93 Alamy Stock Photo:** Panther Media GmbH (bc). **Dreamstime.com:** Yakeyault (br). **Getty Images / iStock:** (bl). **94 Alamy Stock Photo:** Gay Bumgarner (br). **Dreamstime.com:** Anders93 (bl). **95 Shutterstock.com:** Danita Delimont. **98 Getty Images / iStock:** E+ / FG Trade. **100 Shutterstock.com:** samray. **101 Alamy Stock Photo:** Dominique Braud / Dembinsky Photo Associates (bc). **Dreamstime.com:** Gordon Magee (bl). **Shutterstock.com:** Bonnie Taylor Barry (br). **102 Depositphotos Inc:** chasbrutlag (tl). **Dorling Kindersley:** Alan Murphy (cra). **Dreamstime.com:**

Steve Byland (cb); Brian Lasenby (cla); David Pillow (cl); Sue Feldberg (ca); Vasyl Helevachuk (fbl); Mikelane45 (bl). **Shutterstock.com:** Stubblefield Photography (crb). **103 Depositphotos Inc:** Wirestock (fcr). Dorling Kindersley: Tom Grey (bc); E. J. Peiker (fcla); Robert Royse (crb). **Dreamstime.com:** Steve Byland (tc, tr); Isselee (cra); Rck953 (cla); Svetlana Foote (cr); Robmckay (bl). **104 Shutterstock.com:** Edoardo Legnaro. **105 Alamy Stock Photo:** John Van Decker (bc). **Dreamstime.com:** Meunierd (br). **Getty Images:** Moment Open / Image by cuppyuppycake (bl). **106 123RF.com:** Elena Duvernay (cra). **Dorling Kindersley:** Roger Tidman (cl). **Dreamstime.com:** Sue Feldberg (crb); Michael Thompson (cb). **107 123RF.com:** John Bailey / pictur123 (br). **Alamy Stock Photo:** AGAMI Photo Agency / Brian E. Small (cb); Nature Picture Library / Gerrit Vyn (c). **Dorling Kindersley:** Chris Gomersall (tl); Melvin Grey. **Dreamstime.com:** Donyanedomam (clb). **Getty Images / iStock:** Jeff Huth (cra). **108 Getty Images:** Corbis / Buddy Mays (br); Moment / Philip Yabut (bl); Moment / Charmian Perkins (bc). **109 Dreamstime. com:** Isselee (tl). **Getty Images:** John Velocci / 500px. **110 Dreamstime.com:** Steve Byland (b); Rck953 (ca); Mikelane45 (c); Vasyl Helevachuk (clb). **Getty Images / iStock:** MKemalSondas (cra). **Shutterstock.com:** Stubblefield Photography (crb). **111 Dorling Kindersley:** Chris Gomersall Photography (c). **Dreamstime.com:** Farinoza (bl); K Quinn Ferris (bc). **112 Alamy Stock Photo:** blickwinkel / P. Frischknecht. **Dreamstime.com:** Grahammoore999 (bc). **Shutterstock. com:** Ken Griffiths (bl); Nigel Jarvis (br). **114 Dorling Kindersley:** Chris Gomersall Photography (tc, ca, cl); Mike Lane (tr); E. J. Peiker (clb); Roger Wilmshurst (br). **Dreamstime.com:** Farinoza (cr). **Fotolia:** Chrispo (bl). **Getty Images / iStock:** E+ / Gerald Corsi (cla). **Getty Images:** Michael Nolan (cl). **115 Dorling Kindersley:** Roger Tidman (c); Roger Wilmshurst (cra). **Dreamstime.com:** Andreanita (cl); Hakoar (br). **Getty Images / iStock:** Henk Bogaard (cb). **116 Getty Images:** Moment / Vicki Jauron, Babylon and Beyond Photography. **117 Alamy Stock Photo:** dpa picture alliance (br). Dreamstime.com: Menno67 (bl). **Getty Images / iStock:** Tina Horne (bc). **118 Alamy Stock Photo:** Ivan Kuzmin (ftl). Dorling Kindersley: Mike Lane (ca, cb); Roger Tidman (bl). **Dreamstime.com:** Gale Verhague (tl). **Getty Images:** Photodisc / Ed Reschke (c). **Shutterstock.com:** Daniel Danckwerts (cl); R J Endall Photographer (cra). **119 Dorling Kindersley:** Mark Hamblin (cla); David Tipling, Windrush Photos (tl); E. J. Peiker (tr); Steve Young (cra); George McCarthy (cr); Robert Royse (cr). **Dreamstime.com:** Brian Kushner (clb). **Shutterstock.com:** Agami Photo Agency (ca); Gordon Magee (c). **120 Alamy Stock Photo:** blickwinkel / AGAMI / R. Martin (bl). **Dreamstime.com:** Paul

Sparks (bc). **Shutterstock.com:** Andi111 (br). **121 Dreamstime.com:** Wirestock. **122 Dorling Kindersley:** Neil Fletcher (bl); Mark Hamblin (tl); Mike Lane (clb); Roger Tidman (ftl, br). **Dreamstime.com:** Dana Kenneth Johnson (ca); Bill Warchol (cra). Getty Images: Corbis / Gary W. Carter (cr). **123 Alamy Stock Photo:** Nature Picture Library / Claudio Contreras (bl). **Dorling Kindersley:** E. J. Peiker (c); Steve Young (tr); Robert Royse (ca). **Dreamstime.com:** Francisco Blanco (ftl); Gale Verhague (tl). **Getty Images:** Photodisc / Ed Reschke (cl). **Shutterstock.com:** Agami Photo Agency (tc); Donna Bollenbach (cb). **124 Alamy Stock Photo:** imageBROKER.com GmbH & Co. KG / Dieter Hopf (bc). **Getty Images:** Moment / photo by Pam Susemiehl (br). **Shutterstock.com:** Grzegorz Dlugosz (bl). **125 Alamy Stock Photo:** Harry Collins. **126 123RF.com:** John Bailey / pictur123 (br). Dorling Kindersley: Alan Murphy (tc, bl). **Dreamstime.com:** Donyanedomam (cl); Wirestock (tl); Suebmtl (tr); Jgorzynik (cla); Satheesh Rajh Rajagopalan (cr); Michael Woodruff (c). **127 Dorling Kindersley:** Roger Tidman (fbr); Steve Young (cla); Windrush Photos / David Tipling (cr). **Dreamstime.com:** Paul Reeves / Paulreevesphotography (cra). **128-129 Alamy Stock Photo:** Malcolm Schuyl (b). **129 Alamy Stock Photo:** John Cancalosi (tc); Arto Hakola (tl); Minden Pictures / NIS / Steven Ruiter (tr). **130 123RF.com:** John Bailey / pictur123 (cr). **Alamy Stock Photo:** Anthony Pierce (tc). **Dorling Kindersley:** E. J. Peiker (br); Bill Schmoker (tl). **Dreamstime.com:** Brian Kushner (clb); Rebecca Warren (cla). **Getty Images / iStock:** AGAMI stock (bl); Robjem (cb). **131 Dreamstime.com:** Dana Kenneth Johnson (tr); NatmacStock (tl); Wildphoto2 (c); Paul Reeves (cr); Brian Kushner (cb); Mircea Costina / Mirceax (cb); Shawn Mason (bl); Satheesh Rajh Rajagopalan (br). Getty Images / iStock: mirceax (tc). **132 Alamy Stock Photo:** Octavio Campos Salles (bc). **Dreamstime.com:** Birdiegal717 (br). **Shutterstock.com:** Lmimages (bl). 133 **Alamy Stock Photo:** Agami / Brian E. Small. **134 Alamy Stock Photo:** All Canada Photos / Glenn Bartley (clb); Carl Corbidge (fclb). **Dorling Kindersley:** Mike Lane (fbr); E. J. Peiker (tr, cb, crb); Roger Tidman (c); Roger Wilmshurst (fcl, br). **Dreamstime.com:** Birdiegal717 (cl); Brian Kushner (tc, ftr); Brian Lasenby (fcla); Kingmaphotos (cla). **135 Dorling Kindersley:** Chris Gomersall Photography (bl); Mike Lane (ca); Steve Young (cr). **Dreamstime.com:** Byvalet (cra). **Shutterstock.com:** Danita Delimont (cr). **136 Shutterstock.com:** Jarett Thurman. **137 Getty Images / iStock:** (bl). **Getty Images:** Moment / Teresa Kopec (br). **Shutterstock.com:** Heliosphile (bc). **138 Dorling Kindersley:** Tom Grey (cra); Mike Lane (bl); George McCarthy (tc). **Dreamstime. com:** Charles Brutlag (cl); K Quinn Ferris (cla). **Shutterstock.com:** John L. Absher (cb, crb). **139 Dorling Kindersley:** Neil

Fletcher (clb, cb); George McCarthy (tl); Mark Hamblin (ca). **Dreamstime.com:** Kikagogo (cra). **Getty Images / iStock:** Irving A Gaffney (cl); Robjem (tr). **Shutterstock.com:** Agami Photo Agency (bl); Francis Philippe (cr). **140 Alamy Stock Photo:** Pavol Klimek (br). **Dreamstime.com:** Steve Byland (bc). **Shutterstock.com:** Jordan Feeg (bl).**141 Shutterstock.com:** Danita Delimont. **142 Dorling Kindersley:** E. J. Peiker (cr). Dreamstime.com: Steve Byland (ca, crb); Wirestock (cla); Svetlana Foote (tr); Henkbogaard (cl); Matthewo2000 (cb). **Getty Images / iStock:** M. Leonard Photography (fcra); Janet Griffin-Scott (tc). **Getty Images:** Moment / Larry Keller, Lititz Pa. (tl). **143 Alamy Stock Photo:** AGAMI Photo Agency / Brian E. Small (fclb); Johann Schumacher (cla). **Depositphotos Inc:** chasbrutlag (crb). **Dorling Kindersley:** Alan Murphy (cb). **Dreamstime.com:** Rinus Baak (cl); Randy Hjelsand (br). **Getty Images / iStock:** JeffGoulden (tl); Joe Riederer (tc). **Getty Images:** Moment / Grant Glendinning Photography (bc). **Shutterstock.com:** Agami Photo Agency (clb); Annette Shaff (cra). **144 Getty Images / iStock:** WMarissen. **145 Alamy Stock Photo:** Rick & Nora Bowers (bl). **Getty Images:** Moment / Vicki Jauron, Babylon and Beyond Photography (br). **Shutterstock. com:** Jason Yoder (bc). **148 123RF.com:** azoutdoorphoto (bc). **Alamy Stock Photo:** Tom Murphy / Design Pics - Brand B (bl); Andrew Parkinson (br). **149 Alamy Stock Photo:** imageBROKER.com GmbH & Co. KG / Bernd Zoller. **150 Dorling Kindersley:** Chris Gomersall Photography (crb). **Dreamstime.com:** Jeremy Christensen (cra); Outdoorsman (cl); Gregory Johnston (bc). **Shutterstock.com:** Kendall Collett (fclb): Danita Delimont (c); Double Brow Imagery (cl). **151 Alamy Stock Photo:** Papilio / Jack Milchanowski (ftl). **Dorling Kindersley:** Chris Gomersall (fcrb); Mike Lane (crb). **Dreamstime.com:** Steven Blandin (tl); Chris Hill (cl). **Shutterstock. com:** Agami Photo Agency (tr); Wang LiQiang (cb); Nattapong Assalee (bc)

Cover images: Front: **Alamy Stock Photo:** Rolf Nussbaumer Photography br; **Dreamstime.com:** Delmas Lehman tl; **Getty Images:** Darrell Gulin / The Image Bank ca, Jim McWilliams / 500px bc, bmse / Moment tc, Jeff R Clow / Moment cb, Patricia Toth McCormick / Moment Open tr, Annmarie Young Photography / Moment clb; **Getty Images / iStock:** Gerald Corsi / E+ crb; **Shutterstock.com:** skapuka bl; Back: **Alamy Stock Photo:** Tom Reichner br; **Getty Images:** GarysFRP / E+ tc, Michael J. Cohen, Photographer / Moment clb, © Justin Lo / Moment Open tl, Marcia Straub / Moment tr, The Image Bank / Hal Beral crb